WAR IN THE PACIFIC

The most important, explosive, and strategic battles of World War Two took place in the Pacific arena, as the seemingly invincible Japanese sought to expand their notorious empire. Now this astonishing era comes to life in a breathtakingly authentic new series by noted historian Edwin P. Hoyt that places the reader in the heart of the earth-shattering conflict—a dramatic, detailed chronicle of military brilliance and extraordinary human courage on the bloody battlefields of land and sea.

VOLUME
II

STIRRINGS

WAR IN THE PACIFIC

VOLUME II

STIRRINGS

EDWIN P. HOYT

AVON BOOKS ◆ NEW YORK

WAR IN THE PACIFIC, VOLUME II: STIRRINGS is an original publication of Avon Books. This work has never before appeared in book form.

AVON BOOKS
A division of
The Hearst Corporation
105 Madison Avenue
New York, New York 10016

Copyright © 1990 by Edwin P. Hoyt
Published by arrangement with the author
Library of Congress Catalog Card Number: 90-93182
ISBN: 0-380-75793-1

First Avon Books Printing: December 1990

AVON TRADEMARK REG. U.S. PAT. OFF. AND IN OTHER COUNTRIES, MARCA REGISTRADA, HECHO EN U.S.A.

Printed in the U.S.A.

RA 10 9 8 7 6 5 4 3 2 1

CONTENTS

PREAMBLE

The Pearl Harbor attack had left the United States Navy stunned for a moment, but scarcely more. When Admiral Chester W. Nimitz arrived on Christmas Day, his first impression was that Admiral Nagumo had botched the job, and he wondered why, although he was grateful. The Pearl Harbor shore facilities, which (Admiral Yamamoto agreed) should have been in shards, were all intact. And the carrier task forces, which had been at sea at the time of the raid, had also escaped unharmed. The carriers *Lexington* and *Enterprise* were operating out of Pearl Harbor, and the *Saratoga* was at San Diego.

Nimitz paused to read the first statement made by Admiral Ernest J. King, the new commander in chief of the United States fleet:

> The way to victory is long. The going will be hard. We will do the best we can with what we've got. We must have more planes and ships, at once. Then it will be our turn to strike. We will win through—in time.

Nimitz and King had conferred before Nimitz left Washington for Pearl Harbor, and King had given the order to hold a line that ran from Midway to Samoa, Fiji, and Brisbane. So from the outset of the war, Admiral King saw the necessity of protecting the lifeline to Australia and New Zealand, and showed his understanding of the Japanese intent to breach that line.

One thing become apparent quite quickly, and that was that

1

the power of the Pacific Fleet had not been hurt nearly so badly as it appeared at first. Really, only the battleships had been hard-hit, and they were old ships, not really suitable for the war that was thrust upon the navy. They could never stand up to such mighty ships as the *Yamato* and the *Musashi*, Japan's most modern battleships.

From the outset of the war, Admiral King advocated some sort of strike at the Japanese enemy. But Nimitz had the problem of administering the needs of the fleet, and he could not see his way clear to risking so much, so soon, when the fleet was so unready. In January a reported threat to Samoa prompted the reinforcement of that area by marines, escorted by two carrier task forces. Then Admiral Nimitz acceded to Admiral King's request for aggressive action, and the carrier raids against the Japanese-held islands. Actually the first raid was planned by Vice Admiral Wilson Brown, in the command of the carrier *Lexington*, against Wake Island. But it had to be called off when a Japanese submarine sank the task force oiler *Neches* as the force was moving toward its target.

In January the attempt to organize offensive action was again halted when the carrier *Saratoga* was torpedoed by a Japanese submarine and had to go to the West Coast for major repairs and modernization. But the Americans sent ships down to Australia to help organize a defensive force, and Admiral King had hopes of launching an operation against the Marshall Islands off Truk, the big Japanese naval base, to forestall what Admiral King saw as an early attempt by the Japanese to capture Samoa. That was why in late January Admiral Halsey set out to make the raid of the islands of Wotje and Maloelap, to knock out the seaplane bases in the Marshalls while Admiral Frank Jack Fletcher hit the Gilberts and other Marshall islands.

Admiral Yamamoto was aware of these stirrings of activity around the perimeter of the new empire, and he was worried by it. Always in the back of the Yamamoto mind was the picture of an emerging American navy, burgeoning in the might of an American productive capacity, a production power Admiral Yamamoto had observed at first hand in two tours of duty in the United States. These raids on the edges of the empire were one of the reasons that Admiral Yamamoto began thinking of a way to draw the American fleet out of Pearl Harbor and destroy it before the new ships that were being built could begin to join the fleet. Just after the Pearl Harbor attack the Americans had switched; they had been building a number of new cruisers, but most of these hulls were taken over and redesigned to be light aircraft carriers. Admiral Yamamoto did not want to wait until these new carriers were joining the American fleet before conducting his test of strength.

Another great annoyance to Admiral Yamamoto was the raid conducted by the Americans and the Australians against the new Japanese base at Rabaul in February 1942. The idea for the raid had come from Admiral Wilson Brown: that they hit Rabaul and see what happened. So they came down, and Admiral Brown made an approach from the east, hoping to thus avoid interception by the Japanese search planes that fanned out every day from Rabaul to fly 600 miles out to check on the enemy. He intended to launch his planes 125 miles from Rabaul and sneak in behind the search planes, but at 10:15 on February 20 his force was spooked by a bandit, as the enemy is termed, from the north, when the ships were 300 miles east of Rabaul, north of the Solomons. Fighters were sent out from the carrier and they shot down a four-engined flying boat, and then another one, but a third got away, and he must have given the warning. That afternoon at 3:45, the *Lexington*'s radar man picked up a whole flock of bandits out to the west, about 70 miles away. Thus developed the first fight between Japanese and American carrier-type planes, for these Japanese planes were from the Twenty-fifth Air Flotilla at Rabaul.

Admiral Brown launched six more fighter planes to join the combat air patrol, and soon the Japanese came in close to the carrier force, and the fight began.

The fight lasted for nearly two hours, as two waves of nine bombers each attacked and tried to get through to the carrier. The fighters saved the day. Antiaircraft fire from the ships was very inaccurate and did not bring down any planes, a fact that had to be noted unhappily for the eyes of Admiral Nimitz in the action report. But the fighters shot down several planes. Lieutenant Edward H. O'Hare, known as Butch, made his presence known to the world that day by shooting down five enemy bombers single-handedly. Two American fighters and one pilot were lost from the *Lexington*.

But after the battle, Admiral Brown, who was of the old conservative school of commanders, decided that since they had been spooked, he would not carry out the attack on Rabaul, and called it off. During the next two days, February 24 and 25, Admiral Halsey carried out his raids on Wake and Marcus Islands, but the big base at Rabaul went untouched.

Meanwhile the Japanese carrier striking force had raided Darwin, causing heavy destruction, and a pair of long-range flying boats had carried out a raid aimed at Pearl Harbor, which was a complete failure, with one boat dropping its bombs into the sea and the other onto a barren hillside six miles east of Pearl Harbor.

In March 1942, Admiral Brown advised Admiral Nimitz that it was too dangerous to make a raid on Rabaul without at least two carriers. Admiral King made sure he got them—his own *Lexington* and the *Yorktown*, commanded by Rear Admiral Frank Jack Fletcher. King had only one brief order for them: *Attack Enemy*.

The reason for this attack was primarily to cover the American reinforcement of the area, by moving troops to Nouméa from Australia. But as the two carriers were preparing to attack Rabaul, news came of the Japanese landing of troops on Lae and Salamaua on Huon Gulf in that part of New Guinea that faces the Bismarck Sea. This was a part of the overall Japanese plan for the occupation of British New Guinea, called Papua, and was also preparation for the invasion of Australia that the Japanese hoped to be making soon.

There were two methods of response to the Japanese action. One was to move into the Bismarck Sea and then launch planes for air strikes. The other way was to launch from the Gulf of Papua, but that meant flying over the 15,000-foot Owen Stanley Mountains, a very dangerous journey. But it would be equally dangerous to go into the Bismarck Sea, because the water was virtually uncharted, and also it was much closer to the bases of the Japanese Twenty-fifth Air Flotilla, located around Rabaul.

In the end, Admiral Brown decided to send the planes over the Owen Stanley Mountains. Commander W. B. Ault of the *Lexington* air group went first, and from a point above the mountains sent back weather information, orbiting there for several hours. The attack group of 104 planes took off from the carriers. They flew over the mountains, and surprised the Japanese completely. The transports and cargo ships that had brought supplies and troops to Lae and Salamaua were caught. The bombers and the torpedo planes performed nobly, and they hit several ships and sank a minesweeper, a transport, and a converted light cruiser called the *Kongo Maru*. This victory was not parrotted or given much importance, even by Samuel Eliot Morison in his history of American naval operations in World War II, but the fact was that it disturbed the Japanese enormously: it was the first example of American carrier air power, and caused them to redouble their determination to capture New Guinea, and invest the Solomon Islands for their campaign against Australia.

CHAPTER ONE

The "Victory Disease"

Those in Japan who knew or suspected that the Western Allies had been surprised and overwhelmed in the first five months of the Pacific war called what was happening in Tokyo and all the far reaches of the new Japanese empire "the Victory disease." In the five months after December 8 (Tokyo time), the Japanese had captured the Philippines, the Dutch East Indies, and Burma, and had forced Thailand to join the Japanese cause. Hong Kong had fallen, and the Japanese virtually controlled Indochina through their alliance with Hitler's Germany. The American Asiatic Fleet had been destroyed, the American Pacific Fleet battleships had been put out of action, and the British Far Eastern Fleet had been forced to move to the far end of the Indian Ocean. In those five months the white man had been dispossessed from Asia, and his world would never again be the same. Japan controlled Asia from the Indian border to her own island frontiers. She had moved south to the perimeter occupied by Australia and New Zealand. In preparation for future moves the Japanese had also landed troops in British New Guinea, on the Gulf of Huon, and at Lae and Salamaua. To the people at home, Japan seemed invincible, suddenly invincible, after having suffered pangs of envy and unwilling respect for the white man for so many years. Prime Minister Tōjō and the other Japanese leaders vowed that the condition was permanent, and never again would the white man raise his head in Asia—and the Japanese people believed.

Admiral Yamamoto, who was sure Japan had to win a sharp, quick victory or lose the war in a long process of attrition, argued for several moves that would extend the empire and knock out Allied bases. He saw Australia as a major threat, but the army said it could not spare the resources to make an attack on that continent nation. So Admiral Yamamoto contented himself with lesser plans. He argued for an attack on Midway Island, as preliminary to an invasion of Hawaii, which would destroy the American fleet base in the mid-Pacific. He argued for the move into the Solomon Islands to establish naval air bases from which he could interdict air and sea traffic to Australia. He also advocated, after the Doolittle raid on Japan in mid-April, an invasion of the Aleutian Islands, which he felt housed the primary threat to Japan from the air, because long-range bombers could be based there and he knew the Americans were building the B-28 for the specific purpose of bombing Japan.

The Doolittle raid caused the Japanese army to shift its position. As an air raid the Doolittle raid was not much; 16 planes hit Japan, although the original plan had called for 25. And of the 16 planes, 13 bombed Tokyo, unluckily hitting a school and killing 12 civilians. There was virtually no military damage, but the shock was enormous, because the high command had assured the people during the China war that Japan would never be bombed. Admiral Yamamoto, chief of the Combined Fleet, was more shocked than anyone else, and more determined to do something about that raid. One positive result from his point of view was that the army, which had been against Yamamoto's Midway and Aleutians operations, switched, so by the end of April, the plan to draw the American fleet out of Pearl Harbor to Midway and sink the American aircraft carriers was in full motion.

In April 1942, the Americans knew that the Japanese were planning new moves in the South Pacific. The next action was expected to come early in May. Confirmation of this came from the Australians, who reported many Japanese reconnaissance flights over the Coral Sea. Commander Edwin T. Layton, who was the Pacific Fleet Intelligence officer, told Admiral Chester Nimitz that he should expect an amphibious operation directed against British New Guinea. Nimitz then had to decide what he was going to do with his relatively limited forces.

As of the end of April 1942, Nimitz had four carriers available for operations out of Pearl Harbor, but two of them were on their way back from the Doolittle raid against Japan, and could not be immediately employed. The *Lexington* and the *Yorktown* were available, and they were dispatched to the South Pacific Coral Sea area. Admiral Nimitz also moved to establish a South Pacific area command, under Rear Admiral Robert L. Ghormley. The Americans were still not in a very good position to take on the offensive in the Pacific war, but by the end of April they were itching to take it.

The Japanese, who had the offensive, were now preparing to make their second set of moves to extend the empire. This operation was called ''Operation Mo'' by Imperial General Headquarters:

> With the cooperation of the South Seas Army Detachment and the navy we will occupy Port Moresby and important positions on Tulagi and in Southeastern New Guinea. We will establish air bases and strengthen our air operations in the Australian area. Successively an element will carry out a sudden attack against Nauru and Ocean Islands, secure the phosphorus resources located there . . .

Yamamoto placed this whole operation under Vice Admiral Shigeyoshi Inouye of the Fourth Fleet which was located at Rabaul. A great air fleet would soon be based there. Yamamoto had great faith in land-based aircraft as a naval adjunct. Had it not been his land-based aircraft that sank the *Repulse* and the *Prince of Wales* off Malaya at the outset of the war? He told Inouye he would supply land-based air forces. So the orders were issued for a three-part operation. One landing force would head for the island of Tulagi, across from Guadalcanal in the Solomons chain. Another landing force would move against the Louisiade Islands to establish another seaplane base. A bigger force, including 11 transports to carry the troops, would occupy Port Moresby, the main town of British New Guinea. Port Moresby, a copra and fishing port, was of little value except that by controlling British New Guinea, the Japanese could control the skies and seas of northern Australia. The Tulagi landing would be made for the same reason, except that here a seaplane base would be established. The Japanese were very high on seaplanes; they used several types, and found the seaplane version of the Zero fighter very effective, as were the big Kawanishi flying boats. The latter were four-engined planes with an enormous flight range. The boats could bomb, and did, but they were far more valuable as the eyes of the fleet, and gave the Japanese a big advantage in search operations in remote areas.

The Japanese expected opposition from the Americans and Australians in the air, but probably not much on the sea, for they knew of only one aircraft carrier force in the area. They had sent reconnaissance planes over the northern Australian airfields and estimated that there were at least 300 Allied aircraft there capable of action.

The whole operation was under the control of Vice Admiral Inouye, a close friend of Admiral Yamamoto's and a loyal supporter. The plan was announced early but implemented in April as the plans for Midway were being made in Japan. Admiral Inouye learned that he was supposed to take Tulagi, establish the base in the Louisiades, and capture Port Moresby before he would really be ready. The Japanese had been moving so rapidly all spring that their reach was beyond their grasp. The Eleventh Air Fleet would be assigned to Rabaul, but at the moment the area was served by the Twenty-fifth Air Flotilla which could muster only about 45 additional fighters and bombers to be of help in the Solomons and Port Moresby operations. Combined Fleet had assigned support of the landings, first in the Solomons and Louisiades and then at Port Moresby, to Rear Admiral Aritomo Goto, who would have the light carrier *Shoho*. The *Shoho* was a conversion, a carrier of 12,000 tons, but she could only make 24 knots and thus could not keep up with the big carriers which made more than 30 knots. In addition to the *Shoho*, Admiral Inouye was scheduled to have the carrier *Kaga* for this operation, but she was laid up in a shipyard and could not be made ready in time. So Goto would have the one light carrier, plus four heavy cruisers and a destroyer. All these would be close cover, escorting the transports and work ships. Then, ranging freely in the area to give any support that was needed, would be two of the fleet carriers, Admiral Chuichi Hara's Carrier Division Five. The distant cover force was commanded by Vice Admiral Takeo Takagi, and besides the two big fast carriers it consisted of two heavy cruisers and six destroyers.

The invasion of Tulagi and the establishment of the seaplane base would come first. That would give additional air power for the invasion of Port Moresby. Tulagi was to be taken on May 4, then the Tulagi force was to move on, and take Ocean and Nauru Islands, while the Port Moresby force sailed from Rabaul to capture the New Guinea port.

To face this movement the Americans were hard put to assemble a force. Nimitz could send two carrier task forces, one built around the *Yorktown*, and commanded by Vice Admiral Frank Jack Fletcher; the second force, built around the carrier *Lexington*, was commanded by Rear Admiral Aubrey W. Fitch. They were to meet on May 1, east of the New Hebrides Islands, and be prepared to commit their 150 planes to the destruction of the Japanese landings. Nimitz was relying on them, for the army and Australian forces were unknown quantities and the American army pilots still had some training to do.

Admiral Nimitz did not have much else to offer at the moment, except the remnants of the old Asiatic Fleet. Vice Admiral Herbert F. Leary was in the area as commander of "MacArthur's navy," which consisted largely of submarines based at Brisbane, Darwin, and on the west coast of Australia. Rear Admiral J. G. Crace commanded a five-ship force of cruisers, three Australian and two American, that could enter the fight.

Admiral Fletcher, as senior officer of the American forces, would be in command, a prospect that did not much please Admiral Ernest J. King, the chief of the American navy in

Washington; he did not believe that Fletcher had the stomach for a fight. Several times in the past few months, Fletcher had stayed out of possible fights, pleading fueling causes more than any other. It was a reasonable argument in a way, because the Americans were not very good at fueling at sea in these early days of the war and were constantly nervous lest they be caught by the enemy while in the process.

On May 1, the two Japanese covering forces headed out from Truk, and at the same time about 300 miles out of Tulagi, the two American carrier task forces made a rendezvous.

Admiral Fletcher was an old-fashioned man, and he did not have much use for the newfangled radio intelligence systems that everyone at Pearl Harbor was talking about. His carrier and Fitch's both had radio intelligence units aboard, but Fletcher did not pay any attention to the reports of his man. A submarine had been depth-charged that day by American destroyers. What Fletcher wanted to know from his radio intelligence man was whether or not the submarine had managed to send a message to Rabaul, and when the radio officer could not give him an answer, he lost whatever confidence he had. Although the radiomen told him that their information indicated there would be no attack on Australia, Fletcher did not believe it and so he split his force, in defiance of orders from Nimitz. And so the two task forces went steaming away in different directions.

CHAPTER TWO

Tulagi Landing

In Tokyo the euphoria continued, and not just among the uninformed civilians, who were being told that the Japanese army and navy were invincible. The succession of swift victories all over Asia (except in China where the war had settled down to a grim process that was eating away at Japan's resources) persuaded the highest military officials that the Japanese forces were indeed superior to the enemy. The army, having accepted the navy plan for Midway, now wanted to press ahead in the south and extend the perimeter of empire to the very shores of Australia. In the Dutch East Indies, Lieutenant General Imamura was informed—even as he was putting the finishing touches on plans for a government of Indonesia that would turn out to be a real partnership between Japanese and Indonesians—that his next step would be to take over direction of the southern campaign of the Japanese army from Rabaul, where he would command the Eighth Area Army.

From Rabaul small units of Japanese soldiers had fanned out to the many islands, checking on and sometimes arresting the handful of foreigners, missionaries, and planters who lived in these tropical climes. Some of the foreigners were Germans, leftovers from the days when the Bismarck Archipelago and British New Guinea had been German colonies. Some were Australians who were pursued; they escaped for the most part or holed up in the hills. By the beginning of May there were very few Allied nationals still on the loose anywhere in the South Pacific. The Solomon Islands, administered by Australia, had been abandoned with the rush of Japanese conquest, and

Tulagi, an administrative center, was deserted.

On the eighth day of every month every Japanese daily newspaper reprinted the Imperial Rescript declaring war on the Western world, a reminder that the people of Japan must devote their best efforts to achieving victory.

Some newspapers, as they printed the rescript each month, also added observations of their own or also reprinted the poem written by Kotgara Takamura at the height of the ecstasy over Pearl Harbor:

Remember December the Eighth
This day world history has begun anew,
This day occidental domination is shattered.
All through Asia's lands and seas
Japan, with the help of the gods,
Bravely faces white superiority.

All Japanese are soldiers now
Ready to fight
Until the enemy corrects his way.
World history has begun anew.
Remember December the Eighth.

There were some voices of caution, but for public purposes one of them was now missing: that of Admiral Isoroku Yamamoto, who felt that he had done everything possible to avoid this war, and that now that it had come, his task was to support the war as fully as he could in behalf of his beloved emperor.

Another of those who had struggled to avoid war was Shigenori Togo, now foreign minister in the Tōjō cabinet. A few weeks earlier a question had been raised in the Diet about the prospects for peace, now that Japan had attained all she had set out to do. Foreign Minister Togo said that it was equally natural and necessary to stop war as to start it, and he was fully prepared to do whatever he could if the opportunity arose. In fact, he had tried to create an opportunity in his own way, for when Ambassador Sir Richard Craigie was about to be repatriated to Britain, Togo sent his private secretary to see the ambassador and give him a message. If Britain ever decided to make a separate peace with Japan, despite having first followed the American lead, then the Japanese government would be very interested. Togo's statement was heard by the ambassador, but he did not communicate it to his government. What Togo did not realize was the depth of the British-American partnership, which included the agreement that the basic resources of both countries would be turned against Hitler first, but that Japan was not going to get off. Already the Allies were talking about fighting until the enemy gave up in unconditional surrender.

So the Japanese, in the spring of 1942, had a tiger by the tail. They had expanded far in Southeast Asia and the Pacific. Now they had to expand farther to protect their new possessions and prevent the Allies from creating a buildup in Australia to launch a major attack. But even Foreign Minister Togo saw little possibility of a quick end to the war because the Japanese army was pushing forward everywhere. Burma was secure, and Subhas Chandra Bose, the Indian Nationalist leader, was urging Japan to strike and liberate India which would then become a Japanese ally under his direction. Everywhere the call was for Japan to move farther and faster.

Aboard the flagship *Yamamoto* or in Tokyo Admiral Yamamoto made no statements. In early April, when Admiral Nagumo had taken the carrier striking force to hit the British at Trincomalee, he had again failed to knock out the fleet, but Japan was talking about his "great victory" in sinking the carrier *Hermes,* and two other warships. What could Yamamoto say? He was at the Navy Club in Tokyo when the word came of the attack, and Prince Fushimi, a naval officer and member of the royal family, waxed eloquent about the great job being done by the navy. All Yamamoto could do was smile. The victory fever was still in the air, and it would take more than a clear mind and clear eye to the future to change the feelings of the people.

May 7th was the date set for the capture of Port Moresby. Admiral Yamamoto was eager to get his action over with, so that he could get on with his Midway operation. He still smarted from the effects of the Doolittle raid, not because it was a military success—it was a bungled attack, as he put it. What made him embarrassed was that as commander in chief and chief operational officer of the Japanese navy, he took the personal responsibility for the American success in putting any planes at all over Tokyo, and thus threatening the emperor personally. But May 3 was the date for the first landing at Tulagi.

On May 1, Admiral Fitch's *Lexington* task force joined up with Admiral Fletcher's *Yorktown* task force south of Espiritu Santo. Immediately the two task forces started fueling. Admiral Crace's cruiser force was on its way to join them too. Admiral Fletcher's ships fueled first, and so he steamed out into the Coral Sea to try to find the Japanese while Admiral Fitch continued to take on fuel. He was about 200 miles from Tulagi when the Japanese force under Admiral Shima came up to the island and landed. Admiral Goto's cover force stood off New Georgia and the other support group was farther west, with the carriers *Shokaku* and *Zuikaku* off Bougainville, which was well out of the range of Allied search planes just then.

On May 3 Admiral Fitch continued to fuel his ships; he completed the job that afternoon and set out to rejoin Fletcher.

But that afternoon Australia-based aircraft had flown over Tulagi in a routine check and had seen two transports unloading troops and supplies there. They had to be Japanese. Fletcher immediately got into action. He sent the oiler *Neosho* and the destroyer *Sims* to meet Admiral Fitch and direct him to join Fletcher at a point 300 miles south of Guadalcanal Island at dawn on May 5. He then headed north at 27 knots to find the Japanese and strike them with the planes of the *Yorktown*.

Meanwhile, victory fever had spread among the Japanese fleet, and Admiral Goto decided that once the troops and the seaplanes were landed at Tulagi that was the end of the Tulagi operation and he could move on to other matters. So the support groups abandoned their watch about two hours after the landings had been completed at Tulagi. Up north, the two big carriers were sending off planes they had ferried down from

Truk for the Rabaul air force. The Port Moresby invasion force had assembled at Rabaul; the troops were aboard the transports and they were waiting until May 4 to begin their voyage to attack New Guinea. By seven o'clock on the morning of May 4, Admiral Fletcher had reached a point a hundred miles southwest of Guadalcanal. Admirals Fitch and Crace were moving toward the rendezvous, but Fletcher changed his plans, and because they were preserving radio silence as ordered from Pearl Harbor, the other two admirals did not know Fletcher's whereabouts.

Admiral Fletcher ran into stormy weather south of Guadalcanal. A cold front had moved up to Guadalcanal, which made operations rough, but also protected the carrier as it was launching planes.

The Americans were preparing to make a strike, the first to try to wipe out one of the new possessions taken over by the Japanese.

The planes of the *Yorktown* were launched early in the morning, and found the Japanese forces at Tulagi a short time later. Twelve TBD torpedo bombers and 28 SBD dive-bombers came first, and were followed by the launch of six F4F fighter planes for the combat air patrol over the carrier task force.

The Tulagi attack was not a model for the future. In the first place, Admiral Fletcher had only 18 operational fighter planes, which meant that he had no fighters at all to dispatch against the enemy, since he was keeping the 18 for combat air patrol. Thus the attacking bombers would have to defend themselves against attack by the enemy's planes. For this purpose the TBD and SBD were not very well equipped, having only .30-caliber machine guns.

The air squadrons operated independently in these early days, and so they went in. The SBD squadron, commanded by Lieutenant Commander W. O. Burch, arrived over Tulagi first. Down below was Admiral Shima's flagship, a minelayer with a transport and several minesweepers, a number of barges, and two destroyers. The bombers came in with 1,000-pound bombs, and 13 were dropped. One hit the destroyer *Kikuzuki* and damaged her so severely she had to be beached to prevent her from sinking. Two small minesweepers were also sunk by the bombers, which meant that three of the 13 bombs had been effective.

After the dive-bombers had finished, the torpedo bombers came in. Lieutenant Commander Joe Taylor started, and before they were finished the planes launched 11 torpedoes, but sank only the minesweeper *Tama Maru*. Lieutenant W. C. Short arrived with 15 more dive-bombers and these all dropped their bombs, but the damage they did was not observed. Then the planes hurried back to their carrier, to get more bombs and more torpedoes and to refuel. As one pilot recalled, they were in such a hurry they did not even have time to go below and have a cup of coffee.

The second strike consisted of 27 dive-bombers and 11 torpedo bombers. They hit even heavier weather than the first strike on their way to the target, but all planes reached Tulagi safely and came in to attack. By this time the Japanese had all their antiaircraft guns in action and the flak was very heavy around the seaplane base and the ships. The bombers damaged a barge or patrol boat, and destroyed two seaplanes moored in the new seaplane base. Several others were left unhurt. The torpedo bombers attacked the flagship and the other vessels, but the skippers maneuvered and the torpedoes all missed. One of the torpedo bombers ran into difficulty on the way back to the carrier and turned up missing, but there was no indication of any enemy air action.

Two fighter planes were lost when they crash-landed on the coast of Guadalcanal, but both pilots were saved and rescued a few hours later by a destroyer. The fighters found the destroyer *Yuzuki* off Tulagi and attacked her with their machine guns. They strafed the bridge and killed the captain of the destroyer and several crewmen, but the ship itself was not damaged and steamed away out of the action.

A third strike was launched that afternoon, by 21 dive-bombers, but they sank only four landing barges, and before dusk the battle of Tulagi was over.

The day ended, and the pilots gathered in the mess and celebrated their victory. Meanwhile the Japanese at Tulagi had radioed back to Rabaul the news of the attack that had crippled their efforts to set up a seaplane base. Admiral Hara's two big carriers, the *Shokaku* and the *Zuikaku*, had some difficulty that day with weather, which hampered their efforts to fly off the planes they had brought from Truk, and they were too far away to launch planes to find and attack the Americans. So Admiral Hara turned toward the Americans and vowed to launch as soon as possible. The light carrier *Shoho* was detached from its job guarding the Port Moresby force and sent toward Tulagi. But it was too late in the day and nothing could be done.

That night Admiral Fletcher retired into the bad weather that stood above the Coral Sea. Admiral Fletcher was fired up by his pilots' descriptions of their activity. They reported an enormous force of cruisers and destroyers, and said they had sunk several of these. It was very early in the war, and the naval intelligence officers had not yet had much experience in separating the grains of truth from the exaggerated accounts of pilots who saw what they wanted to see as they attacked. So Admiral Fletcher dispatched his two cruisers toward Tulagi to clean up the stragglers. But later in the night common sense prevailed and he brought the cruisers back to the safety of the task force, thus undoubtedly saving them from being sunk by Admiral Hara's bombers, which were launched early and arrived over Tulagi shortly after dawn, to find no trace of the American enemy. On May 5, the two task forces moved toward their rendezvous point, and Admiral Fletcher felt quite secure, so he refueled his ships as they traveled south. That evening, at dusk, the *Yorktown* combat air patrol discovered a four-engine Kawanishi flying boat which was out scouting for the Japanese and they shot it down, but they had to assume that before destruction the pilot managed to radio his position to Rabaul, so they had been discovered. Also, Fletcher's anti-submarine patrol discovered a submarine although it had no chance to attack.

Admiral Fletcher was expecting the air carrier force to head for New Guinea to cover the Port Moresby landings which they knew by radio intelligence would be coming. At this point the Japanese carriers were only 400 miles north of Fletcher's force, which was within Japanese scout plane range although not American. But Fletcher was completely unaware of the danger, and that evening he had a report from Australia about a Japanese convoy steaming through the Louisiade Islands toward the Jomard Passage. This he took to be the major task force, because the pilot of the plane identified a large carrier. Actually what he was seeing was the light carrier *Shoho*. The major task force, with the *Zuikaku* and the *Shokaku*, had passed around the southern Solomon Islands, and was less than 250 miles from Fletcher.

The radio intelligence intercepts were not of much help to Fletcher just then; they were partial messages that were more misleading than anything else.

Admiral Fletcher believed the Japanese carriers were heading for Port Moresby, and that they would soon be attacking bases in Australia, preliminary to the landing at Port Moresby. That had been the original Japanese plan, but when Admiral Hara saw all that he was supposed to do with a two-carrier task force, he had jibbed, and persuaded Admiral Inouye to let him decide when and if he would be able to hit the Australian bases. So Hara was actually looking for the Americans, and prepared to attack as soon as he found them within striking distance. At about 10:30 on the morning of May 3, B-17 bombers moving up from Port Moresby dropped a dozen bombs on Admiral Goto's covering force. They were aiming at the carrier *Shoho* but they did not hit her. Soon the carrier launched fighters, which drove the bombers away. Later that day more Allied planes sighted Admiral Goto's force.

The Japanese now knew that two of their forces had been sighted, and they knew that the Americans were moving into the Louisiade Islands, and expected them to attack the following day, May 7.

On May 6 the two American task forces headed through the Coral Sea, moving toward the Louisiade Islands, which lie between the Solomon Islands and New Guinea. Admiral Inouye knew where Fletcher was, more or less, and where he was heading, and decided to continue operations. By midnight the Port Moresby convoy was very near to Jomard Pass. The seaplane carrier *Kamikawa Maru* was waiting there for them, and overhead the flying planes of the *Shoho* circled until dark. That night the, *Shoho* prepared to launch planes in the morning to cover the operations.

Fletcher always hated surprises and dreaded the thought of ever being surprised. He was confident of having the surprise factor in his court on May 6, but the hope was sadly wrecked on the following morning when the American task force was spooked by a Japanese flying boat at about 10:00 A.M.

On the morning of May 6, Admiral Takagi sent Admiral Hara ahead to try for an air strike that afternoon on the Americans. But the weather turned foul again, and the Japanese planes had to turn back, or the pilots thought they did. Actually if they had persisted they would have broken through the overcasts and found the two American task forces steaming along the Coral Sea underneath sunny, cloudless skies.

So that night at one point, the American and Japanese carrier task forces were only about 70 miles from one another, but neither knew it.

The night of May 6, the carrier force moved on, but the tanker *Neosho* and the destroyer *Sims* were ordered to move back and stay out of the range of the Japanese bombers from Rabaul.

And back at Pearl Harbor and in Washington Admirals Nimitz and King waited anxiously for some word. Because the task forces were observing radio silence, the commands had very little information at this point. Nimitz knew that there had been no clash that day, and hoped that in the fight that was to come the following day, the American forces would be on relatively even terms with the Japanese. That was how it looked from Pearl Harbor on May 6 when Admiral Nimitz turned in for the night.

CHAPTER THREE

Score: Japan 2—U.S. 1

The Coral Sea was a busy place on the morning of May 7, 1942. At dawn the scout planes from the carrier *Yorktown* were out, searching for the Japanese. Admiral Crace's cruiser force was sent forward to guard the Jomard Passage against the coming of the Japanese landing force at Port Moresby.

The Japanese were also up early, searching, and two of their carrier planes discovered the American tanker *Neosho* and the destroyer *Sims* at the fueling rendezvous where they were to wait for the coming of the American carrier task force. The Japanese pilots, like the American, were eager men who tended to overestimate what they were seeing on the surface. They reported back to Admiral Hara that they had spotted part of the American task force, which was true, but they identified the *Neosho* as a carrier and the *Sims* as a cruiser. Naturally Admiral Hara ordered a major attack on this important element of the enemy fleet.

After the Japanese patrol bombers found the Americans and radioed their position, they moved to attack. A single bomb was dropped near the *Sims*, and then the enemy planes disappeared. But half an hour later, 15 Japanese bombers came over the two-ship formation. They bombed from high altitude, missed, and soon disappeared over the horizon. It was about 10:30 in the morning.

Meanwhile the American and Japanese scout planes were still searching for one another's carriers. A *Yorktown* scout bomber shot down a Japanese float plane over Misima Island, about 250 miles from the American carrier fleet, on the edge of Jomard Passage. Reports came from other American planes and from MacArthur's headquarters in Australia about the sighting of two Japanese aircraft carriers in the Jomard Passage area. Like Admiral Hara, Admiral Fletcher believed his pilots and ordered a full-scale air attack from the *Yorktown* and the *Lexington* against the Jomard Island ships. Ninety-three planes got into the air and headed away from their carriers to make the attack. Then at 10:15 the air intelligence officers reported to Admiral Fletcher that a Japanese carrier plane had been sighted very near the fleet. And while he was there, in the plotting office, in came a report from the *Yorktown* scout pilot who had reported the ships at Jomard, correcting the error. What he had sighted were not carriers and cruisers, but two cruisers and two destroyers, he said.

Admiral Fletcher, red with tension, erupted in rage.

"Young man, do you know what you have done? You have just lost the United States two carriers!"

Then Fletcher had to decide whether or not to recall the air strike. While he and his staff were debating the issue, another report came from MacArthur, reaffirming the presence of at least one carrier north of Misima Island, as spotted by a B-17 bomber.

Admiral Fletcher then redirected the air strike to the north of the original target area.

Hardly had that action been taken, when in came a report to the *Yorktown* flag bridge from the *Neosho*. She had just been attacked by enemy bombers, her radioman reported. So Fletcher knew that there had to be two sets of carriers someplace out there. But where?

Admiral Hara was luckier—he knew more about the location of his enemy. His planes had spotted and identified the enemy task force 200 miles south of the flagship *Zuikaku*. But within minutes came two other conflicting reports of task forces: 350 miles to the west, and then 200 miles south, heading for the Louisiade Islands.

So Hara decided to first attack to the south and sent off 76 planes, and then he waited. Soon the reports came back. The targets to the south were only a tanker and a destroyer. At noon 36 dive-bombers from Admiral Hara's carriers appeared over the tanker and destroyer and began their attack. Their primary target was the *Neosho*, which they still identified as a carrier, but some planes attacked the *Sims* and she took three 500-pound bombs, which started fires and exploded in the engine room; soon the *Sims* buckled and broke and sank stern first. When she went down, her boilers exploded, and the ship was lifted 10 feet out of the water and slammed back. The men, trying to escape, were killed by the explosion, and the depth charges also went off. Only about 15 men survived the sinking.

While the *Sims* was dying, the *Neosho* was being battered almost to pieces. Twenty dive-bombers came in to strike. One pilot, hit by gunfire, crashed his plane into a gun station, and the flaming gasoline blazed along the deck. Six other planes made bomb hits and eight near-misses also did damage. Captain J. S. Phillips prepared to abandon ship, and when some of the men heard that order they panicked and jumped over the side. Boats and rafts were lowered to help them, but some were drowned, and others drifted away on the rafts.

The ship was dead in the water, drifting, but her navigator gave the wrong position on the radio, and so when rescuers set out to save the men of the *Neosho* and the survivors of the *Sims*, they searched fruitlessly.

But in the meantime, the fight went on.

Admiral Crace's cruiser force was just west of Jomard Passage when the cruisers were attacked by 11 land-based planes. The ships opened fire and drove off the attackers. Then along came a dozen twin-engined land-based bombers, with torpedoes. By maneuvering frantically the ships managed to escape torpedoing, and shot down five of the bombers. Then came more level bombers, which dropped bombs that missed from high altitude. To add to the confusion, one destroyer of the local American force was also attacked by the Americans, but they did no damage.

After the Japanese planes had attacked the cruisers and found that they were not carriers, Admiral Hara reversed course. Then he had to send signals to his aircraft to tell them where to find the carriers. These signals were picked up by the radio intelligence officer aboard the *Yorktown*: "280 degrees, speed 20 knots."

The radio intelligence officer reported to the admiral's bridge that the enemy was closing in on his force. But Admiral Fletcher had also received a message from Admiral Fitch aboard the *Lexington*, which said something quite different. Fletcher had no great faith in radio intelligence so he chose to believe the *Lexington* report and not his own officer, even though the Americans were traveling at far less than 20 knots and about 200 degrees.

The argument ceased when it was announced that the American air strike had indeed found a carrier north of Misima Island.

Admiral Goto's Port Moresby covering force had been heading southeast for a while, launching planes for combat air patrol and scouting to cover the invasion ships, which were about 30 miles southwest of them.

The 93 planes of the two American carriers were coming.

But that morning of May 7 they did not know where the Japanese were, exactly, or what the Japanese force comprised. The Japanese, from observation planes sent out from Rabaul, knew exactly what the American force consisted of and where it was located. When Admiral Inouye, who was in charge of the entire Port Moresby operation, learned that the Americans were there, he ordered his Port Moresby transports to stop and delay, and not to enter Jomard Passage which would take them toward Port Moresby. He wanted to be sure that the Americans and Australians were dealt with before the transports landed their troops.

At 11:00 A.M. the *Lexington* attack group passed Tagula Island in the Louisiades. One scout plane sighted the carrier *Shoho* and several other warships about 30 miles away. At the same time, the Japanese saw the American planes, and began to move into defensive formation. Two Zeros of the *Shoho* combat air patrol tried to intercept the attack force but were too late. Three American dive-bombers dropped down on the carrier, and one near-miss from a bomb blew five Japanese planes off the flight deck and over the side. Altogether 10 dive-bombers attacked, and a few minutes later along came the *Lexington* torpedo bombers. Less than 10 minutes later, the *Yorktown*'s planes joined the fight. They all concentrated on the light carrier, and soon she had been hit by two 1,000-pound bombs, and went dead in the water. More bombs rained down on her, and torpedoes began to explode against her sides. By 11:30 the carrier was a wreck and her own planes and ammunition were exploding, adding to the carnage. A few minutes later the carrier sank.

"Scratch one flattop," was the laconic message radioed back to the American carriers.

So the carrier planes headed back to the *Lexington* and the *Yorktown*, and the Japanese force, without its carrier, was ordered to make for DeBoyne Island, where it would pick up the *Kamikawa Maru*, a seaplane carrier, which from this point on would have to furnish the air cover.

When the American planes landed and were gassed up and rearmed, Admiral Fletcher had to decide whether or not to make a second strike. His losses on the first had been slight, but he knew there were two big Japanese carriers out there somewhere, not with the group that had been protected by *Shoho*, and he could see that it was possible that he might be engaged with the other carriers before long. So he decided not to make a second strike on the cruisers and destroyers.

That afternoon, Admiral Hara's two carriers came within striking distance of the Americans. At 4:30 in the afternoon, Hara launched 12 bombers, and 15 torpedo bombers took off from the carriers *Shokaku* and *Zuikaku*. They were told that if they found the Americans, they were to wait for sundown and then attack. They did not find the Americans because of very squally weather, and started back for their carriers. They were intercepted by fighter planes from the American carriers, and engaged in several dogfights, in which two American fighter planes were shot down. It was growing dark and the fight took the planes near the American carriers. Several Japanese pilots mistook the American carriers for their own, and three tried to land on the *Yorktown*. The ship's gunner opened fire, and the Japanese planes zoomed away. Then another three Japanese tried to land on the *Yorktown* and one was shot down. The other Japanese planes circled about, trying to find their carrier bases, but the Japanese had no radar, and so the planes were having a difficult time. A number of them ran out of gas and crashed, and fewer than 10 made it back. At the moment this was not vitally important, but it would certainly have its effects later, in preventing either carrier from participating in the Midway battle and in later battles, when the number of trained Japanese pilots was hit harder and harder by attrition.

The Americans really lost a chance to strike the carriers that very day. At 7:30 that evening, the radar man on the *Lexington* spotted blips orbiting in the sky. They were about 30 miles away.

The radar man had the good sense to recognize them as aircraft orbiting a carrier while they waited for their turns to land. He got the word up to Admiral Fitch and Admiral Fitch sent a message to Admiral Fletcher. But someone in communications erred and Fletcher did not get word until 10:00 P.M. and even then he did not believe it. Admiral Fletcher was a real prewar naval man, conservative to the core and usually opposed to new ideas. Anyhow, he reasoned, the Japanese carriers, if they had been there, would be gone by the time a strike could reach out. He was probably right. In any event, he did not take the risk of finding out, and so the Americans lost their chance to hit the enemy hard when he was in the weak position of landing his aircraft. It was the chance of victory missed, for at that time the Japanese were about a hundred miles east of the American carriers and a search most certainly would have found them. Neither did Fletcher risk the detachment of a cruiser force to attack Admiral Takagi's ships although he knew where they were. There were many excuses for this, but the reason was that the Americans were distinctly inferior to the Japanese in night fighting, as would be shown only too clearly in the coming days at Guadalcanal.

Rear Admiral Tamon Yamaguchi looked at the plans with two minds. First, he had been advocating a move into the

Indian Ocean, and the capture of Ceylon. But once he saw the Midway plan, and learned of the Combined Fleet staff's ambitions to capture Hawaii, he became an advocate of Midway. Like Yamamoto, Yamaguchi knew the Americans well, for he had spent a tour as a naval attaché in Washington. He believed, as did Yamamoto, that the American fleet must be decisively beaten before a peace favorable to Japan could possibly be arranged, and Japan did not have much time.

Admiral Kondo had a different point of view. And meeting with Admiral Yamamoto he voiced his concerns. The assault on Midway would have to be made, unlike any previous Japanese landings of this war, without any land-based air support, while the Americans could be expected to have a large air force at Midway. Further, the American carrier force had not been seriously cut down since the beginning of the war—the *Saratoga* had been damaged, but she also had been repaired. So Japan still had to face the American carrier fleet. Kondo suggested that they attack in the South Pacific, to take New Caledonia, and set up bases to break the line of supply between the United States and Australia.

Admiral Yamamoto had an answer for that. What Admiral Kondo urged was precisely what Admiral Inouye was now doing, moving a force to Port Moresby to establish air bases in New Guinea from which the Allied supply lines could be attacked. That was also the purpose of the Tulagi operation, and although the Allies had wiped out the seaplane base, the Japanese still held Tulagi, and it was a question of refurbishing the seaplane base, and perhaps building an airfield on Guadalcanal. No, said Admiral Yamamoto, it was too late to scrap the Midway plan, which had already been approved by the Japanese. Admiral Hara was being told to take his carriers north and cover the transports early in the morning from the air. He headed north and Fletcher headed south, and soon the distance between them was widening rapidly.

Meanwhile, back at the Japanese fleet anchorage at Hashirajima anchorage in Hiroshima Bay, Admiral Yamamoto and his staff were putting the finishing touches on the plan for the attack on Midway Island. Admiral Nagumo's fast carrier force was there, except for Admiral Hara's Division Five; Vice Admiral Kondo's Second Fleet had come back from a wild chase after Admiral William F. Halsey's carrier that had sent the Doolittle raid planes off from waters inside Japan's inner perimeter of empire.

Admiral Nagumo and Admiral Kondo were also studying the plans. Nagumo and his staff, not knowing how low they stood in Admiral Yamamoto's regard, were extremely arrogant and proud of their "accomplishments" at Pearl Harbor, Darwin, and Trincomalee, not knowing that Yamamoto regarded all of them as failures, all caused by Nagumo's timidity and refusal to stick around the target area long enough to finish his job. Nagumo and his staff were the victims of the "Victory disease" as much as anyone in Japan. They believed the propaganda issuing from Imperial General Headquarters about their omniscience and invincibility.

Therefore Admiral Nagumo and his chief of staff merely glanced at the Midway orders and paid very little attention.

The sinking of the carrier *Shoho* had given a shock to Admiral Inouye. This was the first naval setback the Japanese had really encountered. The loss of a handful of small ships in the past had not been too troublesome, except for the virtual fiasco of the first attempts to capture Wake Island, which cost a destroyer and some smaller ships. But until the *Shoho*, nothing larger than a destroyer had gone down, and the Japanese navy, like the army, had begun to feel invincible. The destruction of the Tulagi seaplane base and the loss of the *Shoho* and most of her planes had proved that the Imperial Navy was not indestructible. Admiral Inouye ordered Admiral Goto to send his cruisers and destroyer screen to attack Fletcher's forces. Then Inouye thought twice about the idea, and reversed his order. It would be best to see what happened in the carrier encounter that the Japanese expected the next day. So Inouye ordered the Port Moresby invasion force to go back to Rabaul and wait for two days. By that time the air would be cleared and the next move would be indicated.

Admiral Takagi was getting rather bruised too that night,

because of the loss of so many planes due largely to weather and bad communications between carriers and pilots. His squadron commanders hesitated to send pilots out that night because they were all tired from two days of searches. He contemplated a surface ship attack, believing the enemy was less than a hundred miles away, but before he could make a decision he had a message from Rear Admiral Koso Abe, commander of the Port Moresby invasion force, asking for his support to cover the ships as they returned to Rabaul, now that the *Shoho* had been sunk. So at about the same time that Fletcher was trying to decide what to do, Abe's request to Takagi was the cause of the abandonment of the Port Moresby operation. Meanwhile at Hashirajima Admiral Kondo was looking at the Midway operation in dismay. He wanted it postponed. But Admiral Yamamoto was adamant. The operation had been approved by the navy ministry and Imperial General Headquarters, he said. It would proceed.

So Admiral Kondo went back to his flagship with ruffled feathers, but it did no good.

After the Midway victory, said Admiral Yamamoto, most of the fleet would move to Truk and in July would capture New Caledonia and the Fiji Islands. The carrier force would then carry out a number of raids on Australia. And then in August the carrier force and the fleet would lead transports to capture Johnston Island and Hawaii.

Kondo could rant as he pleased about the Midway plan, but Admiral Yamamoto was obdurate. It was going ahead. Just before the attack force headed for Port Moresby, the officers of the bombing fleet had assembled aboard the flagship *Yamamoto*, for tabletop war games played with Admiral Yamamoto.

The tabletop maneuvers were actually supervised by Admiral Ugaki, the Yamamoto chief of staff. During the maneuver, the Japanese task force was bombed by enemy land-based aircraft, just as Admiral Kondo had suggested they might be. The staff officer who was acting as umpire cast the dice to determine the bombing results. He then awarded the enemy nine enemy hits on the carriers *Akagi* and *Akaga,* and declared them both sunk. But Admiral Ugaki reversed the decision and neither was "sunk." Both appeared in the New Caledonia–Fiji stage of the operations.

During the tabletop maneuvers there was a little rigging done by Admiral Ugaki and could be justified, perhaps, because they were dependent on the fall of the dice, and Ukagi suggested that Japanese skill would play a greater role.

In these games, the Nagumo force did not seem to pay much attention. Rear Admiral Ryunosuke Kusaka was charged with operating the task force recklessly. What would happen, asked a referee, if an enemy task force appeared on the scene while the Japanese force was attacking Midway? Kusaka had not ever considered this possibility. He had better do so, said Yamamoto.

After the exercise, just at about the time the Japanese and American carriers were skirmishing in the Coral Sea, a number of high-ranking officers suggested that the Midway operation and all the rest of it ought to be scheduled a month or two later, to give more time for training. Admiral Ugaki fielded those objections and did not even discuss them with Admiral Yamamoto. Admiral Kusaka suggested that the communications of the *Akagi* were not up to the job, and the flagship, the *Yamamoto*, ought to take over the responsibility. Ugaki dismissed the suggestion.

And so, as the carrier forces in the Coral Sea prepared for battle, at Hashirajima, the Japanese fleet planned the next few months of operations to bring the war to a close.

CHAPTER FOUR

The Carriers Attack

The coming of the small hours of May 6, 1942, found the Japanese and American carrier forces steaming in opposite directions, waiting for dawn and the chance to find and strike the enemy. Admiral Hara's *Shokaku* and *Zuikaku* maintained a course heading north. An hour before sunrise, east and south of the Louisiade Islands, Admiral Hara launched a search mission to the south, reaching out 200 miles.

They had no chance to report back before an hour had passed and Hara launched his first strike of 90 planes heading south. As soon as the last plane was flown off, Admiral Hara increased speed to 30 knots, heading through squalls with the striking force, heading toward the position he estimated the Americans to have reached that morning.

Admiral Fletcher's force had continued to travel southeast all night, and in the morning he awakened to find that he had taken the American carriers out of the bad weather, where they would have liked to be, and into bright open sunshine, with scarcely a cloud in the sky.

That morning Admiral Fitch's *Lexington* was given the job of conducting the search for the enemy. Eighteen scout bombers were launched at 6:25. Two hours went by, without a word, and then one American pilot caught a glimpse of Hara's ships down through the overcast. A few minutes later he reported to the carrier, giving the enemy course, speed, and position, which was about 175 miles northeast of the *Lexington* and *Yorktown*. Another pilot, Lieutenant Commander R. F. Dixon, then corroborated the first pilot's findings, and the hunt was on. Dixon spotted and trailed the enemy for an hour, but then his fuel supply ran down and he had to turn back to his carrier.

Meanwhile, as soon as Admiral Fletcher had heard of the first pilot's report, he ordered the air strike launched. Also, recognizing that Admiral Fitch was a far better airman than he was, Fletcher turned over tactical command of the operation to Fitch.

At 9:15 the *Yorktown*'s 39 attack planes were in the air and flying toward the enemy. An hour and three-quarters later, they found the Japanese. There below were the *Shokaku* and the *Zuikaku*, each screened by two heavy cruisers and several destroyers. The carriers were about 10 miles apart then.

The faster American dive-bombers reached the area first, and found cloud cover and hung out there, waiting for the torpedo planes to arrive. Down below they could see the Japanese launching fighter planes to strengthen the combat air patrol they would have to fight through. Then the *Zuikaku* disappeared into a rain squall.

Finally, just before eleven o'clock, the *Yorktown*'s torpedo bombers, Torpedo Squadron Five, came up under Lieutenant Commander Joe Taylor and were prepared to attack. They headed for the *Shokaku* while the American fighters prepared to do battle with the Zeros coming up from the Japanese carrier.

Torpedo Squadron Five was too anxious. The planes came in, but began to launch torpedoes before they got into proper range, so many of them missed, and although the Americans did not yet know it, the aerial torpedoes, like the American submarine torpedoes, were inclined to misfire, or not explode at all, due to an inferior exploding mechanism copied from the Germans. So the score for the *Yorktown* torpedo bombers was nil, and three of her planes were shot down by antiaircraft fire.

Bombing Five did better. At least two bomb hits were scored on the *Shokaku* and these were lucky hits because they started fires that damaged the *Shokaku* so that she could not launch any more planes. Actually the fires looked worse than they were in terms of the ship's safety, and when Admiral Hara, in his flagship *Zuikaku*, emerged from the rain squall he was astonished to see his other carrier burning furiously and apparently in deep trouble.

The *Lexington*'s air strike had even more trouble. Shortly after the strike got going, the three fighters that were escorting the dive-bombers got lost and finally ended up returning to the carrier. The torpedo squadron went to the wrong place, and then had to fly a search pattern to find the right place. The dive-bombers never did find the Japanese carriers, and finally had to start home because they were running out of gasoline. So the *Lexington*'s attack was made by 11 torpedo bombers, five dive-bombers, and six fighter planes. The torpedo planes came down out of the clouds from 6,000 feet. The dive-bombers were preceded by the fighters, which ran into serious opposition from the Zeros, and three of the American fighters were shot down.

The torpedo attack was ineffectual, and although the Americans did not realize it, the main reason was because the planes they were using were just too slow for the job. As a Japanese officer said, "We could turn and run away from the torpedo bombers." So there were no torpedo hits, but the *Lexington* dive-bombers did manage to make one more bomb hit on the *Shokaku*.

The damage seemed spectacular, and the Americans began talking about seeing a carrier settling in the water. But the fires, while killing and wounding 150 men, were soon brought under control, there were no hits below the waterline, and the carrier was all right. Her planes were told to land on the *Zuikaku* when they came in.

At about the same time that the American planes were making their attack on the two Japanese carriers, the Japanese planes found the American carriers.

The Japanese were smart and lucky. They spotted American planes heading back south and realized that these aircraft must be making for the American carriers. Admiral Hara's strike force followed the Americans, and the American planes led them to the carriers.

Furthermore, the Japanese now were far more experienced than the Americans in actual carrier warfare; they had been employing their carriers in China waters since 1937—more than four years. The Japanese attack was well-coordinated and accurate. Just before eleven in the morning, Admiral Fitch sent aloft every fighter and dive-bomber he could put into the air.

At 10:55 the radar operators of the carrier *Lexington* picked up the blips of a large group of aircraft heading toward their carrier, about 70 miles to the northeast. The position of the carrier was awkward. One group of planes on patrol had just been recovered, and only eight fighters were above the carriers giving combat air patrol protection, and they were too low on gas to be sent out to meet the invaders, even if there had been enough of them, so they were ordered to stay above the ships and protect at close range any who got through soon. The carriers then were ordered by Admiral Fitch to change course, and to speed up. They headed to the southeast and began launching fighters. Five of the fighters were sent out forward to try to stop the Japanese, but everybody knew that it was a hopeless mission, and probable suicide for those fighters. But it did not quite work that way. Two of the fighters flew down low on the deck, to intercept torpedo planes, but the Japanese fighters kept after them, and three others flew at 10,000 feet, which showed how little they knew about the Japanese attack pattern, because the Japanese were above them, reached their attack position, and went down. Four other fighters missed the action altogether. So one might say that the fighter interception of the Americans against the Japanese attack was almost a complete failure.

The Americans learned fast, but they had a lot to learn.

The Americans did not have enough fighter planes to protect their carriers; it was as simple as that. The Wildcat fighter then in use was not the equivalent of the Japanese Zero, but it was a good aircraft and if piloted skillfully could make a good showing for itself. But the SBD dive-bomber was very slow compared to the Japanese fighters. Still, Admiral Fitch had to use them in his defense. And he did employ 23 dive-bombers as defense planes that day. They did not have adequate armament either, and so the odds were bad. Four of them were shot down in the next hour, although the bombers did shoot down four Japanese torpedo planes.

But the main line of defense for the carriers that day had to be the antiaircraft guns.

Just after 11:15 that morning the Japanese came in sight from the northeast and approached both bows of the *Lexington*. When the torpedo planes were three-quarters of a mile from the carrier, they began to launch their torpedoes.

The first plane was literally blown out of the air by the American antiaircraft gunners, but there were too many planes, and the approach was calculated to get hits. Captain Frederick Sherman ordered the *Lexington* turned sharply to the right, but then in came two more planes on the starboard bow, and these were followed by more on both sides. It was impossible to maneuver the carrier to miss them all, and two torpedoes struck on the port side, one forward and one opposite the bridge.

Because all the American fighters and the dive-bombers were down on the deck trying to drive off the torpedo bombers, there was no interference to the attack by the Japanese Aichi 99 dive-bombers when they came hurtling down from 17,000 feet and then bombed and pulled up at about 2,000 feet. One bomb exploded on the port side of the *Lexington*'s main deck, in a box of five-inch antiaircraft ammunition, which then exploded as well. Another bomb hit on the stack, and still others missed so nearly that they buckled planes and wounded men.

The *Lexington* was the primary target, but some torpedo planes and bombers also went after the *Yorktown*. She was luckier, or her attackers were less skillful, because they did not use the technique of attacking on both bows simultaneously and the skipper and helmsman were able to turn away from the torpedo planes as they came in.

But just before 11:30 the dive-bombers came after the *Yorktown*, too, and soon bombs were dropping all around her. One 800-pound bomb struck the flight deck, near the island, and went down to the fourth deck before it exploded. More than 60 men were injured or killed and many fires started. But soon the damage control parties had the fires under control. Flight operations continued all the while.

The Japanese attackers left then, and hurried back to their single carrier, for Admiral Hara had sent the damaged *Shokaku* back to Truk and so the returning planes were taken aboard by the *Zuikaku*. The pilots reported that they had sunk both carriers and left a battleship or cruiser burning. In fact, as of that moment, they had sunk nothing, but had damaged both American carriers.

There was room for the *Shokaku* planes on the *Zuikaku*, because the Japanese losses were quite heavy. Thirty planes were lost in the attack on the two carriers, and another 13 were lost in operational mishaps, accidents in landing, or lost at sea.

At noon Admiral Fletcher was jubilant. It seemed that the Americans had gained a victory, sinking one small Japanese carrier and damaging another, with damage to two carriers, but both remaining operational. The *Lexington* was listing but her flight deck was soon made operational again, and by shifting ballast the list was corrected. The damage control officer reported that the ship would soon be "back on an even keel."

But then uncertain fate took a hand. The torpedo hits and perhaps some of the near-misses by bombs had loosened the plates in some of the fuel compartments, and a motor generator running below deck ignited the fumes, and an enormous explosion shook the carrier from one end to the other. It was 12:47 and back at Pearl Harbor Admiral Nimitz had just finished registering a victory for the fleet in the war diary. Explosions followed, knocking out the central communications system and rupturing many water lines which prevented the fire fighting from being very effective. Smoke began to pour out of the lower decks.

But the *Lexington* was continuing to operate her flight system, and the planes from the morning mission were recovered one by one until at 2:14 in the afternoon, the last plane was on deck. The ship was still making 25 knots although three of her boiler rooms were flooded. Even after that major explosion no one was thinking of abandoning her.

Then at 2:45 came another internal explosion, again caused

by gasoline fumes, and this one wrecked the ventilation system of the ship's engine rooms. Captain Sherman called for other ships to come alongside and help with the fire fighting because the *Lexington*'s water system was no longer capable. The destroyer *Morris* came alongside and put hoses aboard the carrier, but it was not enough; the plates of the ship in the lower compartments were growing red-hot.

Captain Sherman assembled all the information. He ordered the sick and wounded to be moved off the ship into its boats. Flying squadron personnel except for the pilots had gone over the side to the destroyer *Morris*. Captain Sherman then reassessed the situation and found it extremely grave. The warheads of the torpedoes in stowage had heated up to 140 degrees, and he was afraid they would start exploding at any moment. The bomb stowage compartments were very near the fires. He was afraid the whole ship might blow up at any moment.

So Sherman ordered the engine room crews to close down and come up to the top deck. They cut off the fires and drained the steam lines and the ship coasted to a stop. At 4:30 in the afternoon he ordered the men to prepare to abandon ship. Rafts were cast loose, and search was made of the compartments below to be sure no sick or wounded had been left behind.

Just after five o'clock Captain Sherman and Admiral Fitch agreed it was time to get the men off the carrier. Rear Admiral Thomas Kinkaid in the cruiser *Minneapolis* took charge of rescue operations, and the sailors and marines began going over the side on lifelines, and dropping into rafts for the most part. The destroyers *Hammann*, *Morris*, and *Anderson* came alongside and picked up men from the rafts and the sea. The water was calm and warm, and the whole procedure was carried out slowly and methodically. There was so much time that one group of sailors, awaiting their turn to go over the side, stopped by the ship's service store and ate the ice cream there. Not a man and not even Captain Sherman's pet dog was lost in the abandonment.

Admiral Fitch transferred his flag to the *Minneapolis*; Captain Sherman made one last inspection of the ship, and while he did so she was shaken by still another big internal explosion.

There was no one left aboard except a corporal of marines, the ship's executive officer, and himself. They went over the side then, and slid down the lines into the sea, where they were picked up.

Admiral Fletcher watched the *Lexington*, dead in the water, smoke coming from her fires, and he gave the order to have her sunk by torpedo from a destroyer. The destroyer *Phelps* had the job. She fired torpedoes, and at about eight o'clock that night the *Lexington* sank in deep water.

So what had been a victory all around for the Americans was now a defeat. They had lost one of their major carriers and had cost the Japanese only one small carrier and damage to another. Even as they steamed along that night the radio intelligence officers were listening in to the Japanese ship talk, and learned that the *Shokaku* was not very badly damaged and that she was going to Truk for repairs.

That afternoon, when Admiral Fletcher reported that the *Lexington* was in bad shape and had to be abandoned, at first Admiral Nimitz objected, but then he reasoned that the men on the scene might know better than he. Certainly Admiral Fitch would never have let his flagship go had it not been absolutely impossible to save her. So Admiral Nimitz ordered Admiral Fletcher to turn around and head for Pearl Harbor. He had news that indicated that he was going to need every carrier he had in the near future to fend off a new Japanese attack. Radio intelligence had indicated that Admiral Yamamoto was planning something big, probably an attack and invasion of Midway Island, and if that was the case, then Admiral Nimitz was going to have to send the fleet out to save the vital submarine base.

That night, at about 6 P.M., Admiral Inouye ordered Admiral Takagi to take the protective force, including the carrier *Zuikaku*, back to Truk. He considered the problem of the invasion of Port Moresby, and finally decided that it must be postponed until after the Midway invasion operation, because he did not have any carriers left to protect the invading troops. The *Shoho* was sunk, the *Shokaku* was damaged, and besides, both she and the *Zuikaku* were scheduled to be returned to Japan to engage in the Midway operation. Without carriers, he did not want to risk his ships, even though he thought both American carriers had been sunk. But the American and Australian land-based planes had also been giving the Japanese a very hard time in the past few days, and so Inouye decided against further operations for the moment and ordered the Port Moresby ships to go to Rabaul and stay there until further notice.

When Admiral Yamamoto had the news of the battle of the Coral Sea, he was not very happy. He had been told that the two American carriers were sunk (which he only half-believed) but what about the other ships? He ordered Admiral Takagi to turn around and go after the rest of the American fleet. So they turned, and headed back toward where Fletcher had been, but Fletcher was moving toward Pearl Harbor now and no contact was made. Two days later Yamamoto gave up and ordered the ships back to Truk.

That day, May 20, the invasion force that was scheduled to take Ocean Island and Nauru left Rabaul, but was scarcely at sea when the flagship, the *Okinoshima*, was sunk by an American submarine. A few days later a patrol plane reported two American carriers heading for the South Pacific. This was Admiral Halsey's force, which was coming to help Fletcher, but the *Enterprise* and the *Hornet* did not get to the Coral Sea but operated for a few days off Santa Cruz before returning to Pearl Harbor at Nimitz's call. All this while the information coming in by radio intercept was confirming the news that an enormous battle was shaping up.

So the battle of the Coral Sea was over, and it had changed from what it seemed to be, first an American victory in the sinking of the *Shoho*, and then an American defeat in the loss of the *Lexington*, and finally a sort of draw, because Admiral Hara had not followed up his victory and attacked the *Yorktown* a second time. The loss of the *Lexington* was a serious blow to an America short of carriers. As the writer Hanson Baldwin put it, the U.S. was fighting a seven-ocean war with a one-ocean navy.

But to the Japanese, the loss of the pilots and planes of the *Shoho*, and many of the pilots and planes of the *Zuikaku* and the *Shokaku*, was equally serious because the Japanese pilot training program was very slow, and had not been altered since the war began. Japanese pilots were superb, but it took almost five years to make them that way. The Americans, starting with a small naval force, had realized that they would have to train men in a hurry and were evolving programs to make a pilot in a year. So strategically the battle of the Coral Sea was an American victory, although at the moment the situation was so confused that both sides were claiming victory and inflating the losses of the other.

CHAPTER FIVE

Nimitz Smells Something Fishy

Because of the radio intercepts and the ability of the Pearl Harbor radio intelligence team to translate at least part of the Japanese messages, the Americans soon knew that the score at the Coral Sea had been better for the U.S. than the Japanese were admitting. Radio Tokyo announced a tremendous victory, but the Americans had nothing to say about it. They were not going to compromise their intelligence operation.

The radio intelligence bits and pieces kept coming in. In April the Japanese navy had revealed an enormous interest in maps of the Aleutian Islands. The commander of a Japanese battleship told Admiral Yamamoto he would not be able to take his ship in the new campaign because it had to go into dockyards for a refit.

Listening to the radio traffic, the fleet intelligence officers became convinced that something serious was up in the mid-Pacific. They did not know where and they were not sure when, but it seemed to be moving fast. Nimitz was convinced soon enough that something was fishy, a fact he suggested in his war diary. Soon it became evident that whatever was planned was coming just after the first of June.

Commander Joseph Rochefort, the Pacific Fleet radio intelligence officer, suspected that what was going to happen concerned the Central Pacific, not the South Pacific. And by decrypting messages from the Japanese submarine force headquarters at Kwajalein, Rochefort learned that they were talking about a second AK operation, and he knew that AK was the Japanese designation for French Frigate Shoals, and AH was Pearl Harbor. Earlier they had sent submarines to French Frigate Shoals not far away, where they sent submarine-carried aircraft over Hawaii for observation. So they were going to do it again. Nimitz then ordered a minelayer sent to French Frigate shoals to discourage the Japanese from trying any such operations.

All this was supposition, but it happened to be correct supposition. Admiral Yamamoto, ready to launch his attack on Midway, needed to know the whereabouts of the American fleet, and particularly the carriers, so he wanted that flight over Oahu.

Following the Coral Sea battle, some Japanese naval officers wanted to delay the Midway operation until the *Shokaku* and the *Zuikaku* could be repaired and their air contingents brought up to strength. But the primary consideration was weather and tides, and they dictated that the Midway and Aleutians operations must be done in the first week of June. After that the Aleutians would be hidden behind layers of fog, and at Midway they would have to face high water at high tide in order to get over the reef surrounding the atoll. Delay would mean delay for many months, because the Imperial General Headquarters had an inflexible timetable for conquest in the South Pacific.

Yamamoto had decided to employ the entire Combined Fleet for this operation, the idea being to thus lure the American Pacific Fleet to Midway and then destroy it.

At Coral Sea the *Lexington* had been lost and the *Yorktown* had suffered damage that would probably take three months to repair, said Admiral Fletcher. That meant that at the moment, the Americans only had the *Enterprise* and the *Hornet* in the Pacific. The *Saratoga* was still on the West Coast being repaired from her torpedo damage, and the *Yorktown* was on her way to dry dock in Pearl Harbor.

So the Japanese carriers outnumbered the American carriers by five to one, which gave Admiral Yamamoto a comfortable feeling, and Admiral Nimitz a very uncomfortable one.

This unease was heightened when Admiral King displayed

an attack of the jitters about the slender carrier force and suggested to Nimitz that he might want to put the carriers and their groups ashore in the South Pacific, keeping the carriers themselves out of harm's way. Thus the entire concept of mobility would be sacrificed. King's intelligence people in Washington were convinced that the South Pacific would be the scene of the next action, and the Japanese messages ordering the occupation of Nauru and Ocean Islands convinced them of that fact. Nimitz had sent Halsey down to stop that, but on King's orders Halsey was recalled because King did not want to risk the two carriers outside the cover of land-based aircraft.

In the second week of May Commander Rochefort's staff deciphered messages indicating that the *koryaku butai* (invasion force) was going to move in on AF. This sort of message had been sent just before the invasion of Rabaul and Java so the Americans knew it meant invasion. But where was AF? That was the stopper.

Rochefort was certain that AF was Midway, but in Washington the intelligence officers did not believe it and they kept telling Admiral King that the invasion was going to be at Johnston Island, another American Pacific outpost. But Washington went even further, and suggested that the Japanese might be preparing to invade the American West Coast. At Pearl Harbor this seemed laughable, for the staff there knew the extent of the Japanese commitment of men and material in China and the Pacific, and they knew that Japan simply did not have the men and equipment to invade the American continent. Indeed, in Japan the big question being asked by opponents of the Midway operations was how were they going to supply Midway and the Aleutians after they were captured? And no one had answered that question.

Nimitz then faced an enormous problem. He needed to bring together all of his resources if he was to combat the Japanese effort against Midway, and he knew that the battleship *Hiei* was going to be employed, so he could assume that other battleships would also be along. But in Washington Admiral King did not believe the target was Midway and his intelligence officers were insisting that the Japanese were going to move south, not east. That meant New Caledonia and Fiji, and Admiral King did everything but order Nimitz to send the carrier planes from the *Enterprise* and the *Hornet* ashore to protect New Caledonia. Nimitz resisted. He did assure King that he would keep the carriers outside the range of the land-based Japanese bombers, but he insisted that he must keep them mobile to counteract any Japanese threat anywhere.

Thus Admiral Halsey was told by Nimitz to make a feint toward the South Pacific and make sure he was observed by a Japanese aircraft, and then to turn and hurry back to Pearl Harbor. Halsey did just this. Because of it, Admiral Inouye announced the indefinite postponement of the invasion of Nauru and Ocean Islands, so that he could concentrate his land-based aircraft and ships at Rabaul on wiping out the American task force that was supposedly heading his way.

At Pearl Harbor the deciphered messages piled up, and among them were requests for maps of various parts of Hawaii. So again, the radio intelligence men knew that the Japanese were planning the Midway invasion as a step toward the occupation of the Hawaiian Islands. The evidence just kept building up.

Finally Admiral King was convinced that Nimitz was right and accepted the need to defend against an attack on Midway. Nimitz then ordered the reinforcement of Midway with aircraft and submarines, and the dispatch of a force to Alaska. The carriers *Hornet* and *Enterprise* were on their way to Pearl Harbor and so was the *Yorktown*, which had stopped off at Nouméa after the Coral Sea battle and Fletcher had revised his repair time downward from three months and announced that it could be done at Pearl Harbor instead of the West Coast. Nimitz then became hopeful that the repairs could be expedited and he would have three carriers to send to Midway.

The next problem was to discover from the radio interception what the Japanese battle plan would be. This was very important because even with three carriers, the Americans would be badly outgunned by the Japanese carriers. The positive factor was the existence of the land-based air force on Midway, which was being strengthened.

In spite of the fact that the Japanese did not know the Americans had broken their naval code, the Japanese navy was very careful about issuing instructions: no single message carried the complete operational orders for the Midway invasion. To the Americans it was like working out a jigsaw puzzle, fitting pieces together until a picture emerged. They soon discovered that the Japanese were referring to N-Day, and that Admiral Nagumo's carrier striking force was to begin operations against Midway two days before N-Day.

So when was N-Day?

By taking bits and pieces of messages, Commander Rochefort came to the conclusion that N-Day was going to be June 3. But once more the intelligence officers in Washington disagreed, and told Admiral King that N-Day was going to be in mid-June. So once more Nimitz was stymied.

Then came the brilliant suggestion by Lieutenant Commander Jasper Holmes, one of Rochefort's staff. He knew that Midway's water supply came from evaporator plants. He suggested that messages be sent in the clear or in code known to the Japanese (captured at Wake Island) saying that Midway was short of water and calling on Pearl Harbor to send barges laden with water. Immediately the Japanese reacted, sending messages indicating that their advance air unit, which was to accompany the invasion, would need two weeks' water supply to go along. So then Nimitz knew that the invasion was planned for before June 15, the day Washington was figuring it for.

Time was growing short. Halsey was due in Pearl Harbor on May 26, and Fletcher's damaged *Yorktown* was not due until May 27, and would then have to be repaired—if it could be done in time—and then the task forces would have to move out and head for Midway.

But they still did not know the date set for the Japanese invasion.

So Nimitz gambled and made his plans to get those task forces off Midway by June 1 if possible. The *Saratoga* could not be counted on; she would not leave the West Coast until

June 5. The *Yorktown* must be repaired in time.

Finally Commander Rochefort had a breakthrough and ascertained from several messages that the date of invasion was going to be June 4.

Then Halsey arrived. Nimitz had expected to put him in charge of this operation, but Halsey was sick with dermatitis and was unable to function in command. He had to go into the hospital. He recommended that his place be taken by his cruiser commander, Rear Admiral Raymond Spruance, and Admiral Nimitz agreed. But that meant that Admiral Fletcher would be in charge because he was senior naval commander next to Halsey.

A final staff meeting was held in Nimitz's office; he was told that the Japanese would attack Midway on June 4, early in the morning, coming from the northwest.

The orders were issued and the work begun on the repair of the *Yorktown* on a 24-hour basis using every man that could be squeezed aboard the carrier.

Nimitz inspected the damage himself, and ordered minimal repairs to be made to make her seaworthy in a hurry for the coming battle. A patch was welded to the hull, and weak bulkheads were shored up with timbers. It had to be done in three days, Nimitz said, and 1,500 men got down to work.

"We must have the ship back in three days," Nimitz told the engineers.

On the 28th of May, the Japanese changed their naval code, which blocked out the information received by the Pearl Harbor radio intelligence for the time being. They had all the information they were going to get about the Midway operation.

The next step of the Americans was to engage in some radio deception to prevent the Japanese from finding out what they wanted to know—the whereabouts of the American aircraft carriers. On May 28, Admiral Spruance took Halsey's Task Force Sixteen and headed for a point about 350 miles northeast of Midway. Meanwhile down in the South Pacific, the seaplane tender *Tangier* began broadcasts which simulated an American aircraft carrier on routine flight operations. In the Coral Sea, the cruiser *Salt Lake City* did the same thing. These broadcasts were aimed to convince the Japanese that the American carriers of the Halsey force were more than a thousand miles away from Midway. The Japanese heard the messages and believed. During the early part of May the Japanese were assessing the battle of the Coral Sea and preparing for Midway. Admiral Yamamoto's flagship, the *Yamato*, left the fleet anchorage at Hashirajima and went to Kure to load supplies and make repairs of minor breakdowns. Ships kept arriving and leaving constantly. The carriers *Ryujo* and *Junyo*, which were assigned to the Aleutians invasion force, loaded up winter clothing and equipment.

On May 18, Colonel Kiyonao Ichiki, who was the commander of the specially trained army detachment that would occupy Midway Island, went aboard the flagship for a briefing and conference with Admiral Yamamoto.

The Ichiki briefing ended the preparations, and on May 19 Admiral Yamamoto returned to Hashirajima to make preparations for the attack. From submarine and other intelligence the Japanese discovered that the Americans' Midway defenses included 750 marines, about 24 flying boat patrol bombers, 12 army bombers, and 20 fighters, and a number of patrol boats and submarines operating off the atoll.

What the Japanese really wanted to know was the whereabouts of the American aircraft carriers. They believed the *Hornet* and the *Enterprise* were in Pearl Harbor, having arrived back from the Tokyo raid. They now estimated that only one carrier was sunk at Coral Sea and that the other was probably at Hawaii. They wondered where the carrier *Wasp* was; they had lost track of it. They were sure the *Ranber* was operating in the Atlantic. They now knew that the *Saratoga* had not been sunk off Hawaii by a Japanese submarine, but only damaged, and was undergoing repairs. That accounted for the two American carrier forces after the sinking of the *Lexington*, except for some escort carriers that had been finished recently, but these were not regarded as a threat since they were very slow and small.

But most recently the fleet headquarters had been told about the sighting of two carriers east of the Solomon Islands, which meant that the *Hornet* and the *Enterprise* might not be at Pearl Harbor, and if that was the case, then the Americans would have no more carriers to oppose the Japanese at Midway. That would make the invasion easy, but would wreck Yamamoto's hopes of drawing the American fleet into a decisive battle and defeating the fleet.

In the last days of May, the Japanese were moving. The transport group, which would take the landing forces to Midway, sailed for Saipan, the assembly point for the invasion forces. The northern force, headed for the Aleutians, also moved out to Honshu waters.

On May 25, Admiral Yamamoto once again held tabletop maneuvers, in which the invasion of the Midway atoll was simulated.

Also on May 25 all the forces were assembled: the northern Aleutians force at Ominato in northern Honshu Island, and the others at Hashirajima, at Saipan, and at Guam.

At noon on May 26 the Second Carrier Striking Force, commanded by Rear Admiral Kakuji Kakuta, left for the Aleutians, heading through fog, toward Dutch Harbor, Alaska, for their first strike. They would reach their destination by June 4.

On May 27, Admiral Nagumo's First Striking Force left Hashirajima anchorage, 21 ships strong, moving through the Bungo Strait into the Pacific and heading southeast.

On May 28 the Attu and Kiska invasion forces moved out from northern Japan, and the Midway landing forces sailed from Saipan, guarded by a cruiser, the *Jintsu,* and a dozen destroyers and the seaplane cruiser *Chitose.* Admiral Kurita's support group of heavy cruisers sailed from Guam.

Last to leave for Midway was Admiral Yamamoto's main force of 32 ships, light cruisers, cruisers, and destroyers, and battleships, with the light carrier *Hosho* along for air cover.

The sailing of the main force of the Combined Fleet represented a return to the old battleship tactics. The men of the battleships expected to meet the American big ships in gun battle and to defeat them, particularly with the big new battleship *Yamato* with the heaviest guns in the world. Seven battleships in all steamed out to find the enemy, moving south-east at 18 knots in two columns.

May 29 found the Japanese forces moving along toward their objectives, but that day the weather began to turn rough and on May 30 the wind and rain grew stronger, and the big ships were taking water over the bows. The formation speed was cut to 14 knots.

That day the radio officers aboard the flagship were distressed to discover a long urgent message sent by a submarine that was directly ahead of their course. Yamamoto's staff suggested that the transport group had been discovered. But they were not worried. Did not their plans call for them to draw out the American fleet from Hawaii? If this message reached the enemy fleet and they came out, then all the better; the mission would have been accomplished.

May 31 brought more bad weather to the Japanese fleet. This day it affected even the carriers which were several hundred miles farther east than the battleships and cruisers.

Admiral Yamamoto was now waiting for reports from two flying boats, for he had ordered them up to Wotje, and then to French Frigate Shoals, where they would refuel from submarines and then fly over Hawaii to see where the American carriers were actually located.

Although Admiral Yamamoto did not know it, his plan had miscarried because of Admiral Nimitz's order to send a ship or two to French Frigate Shoals after the radio intercepts had indicated the Japanese plans. The submarine scheduled to refuel the flying boats arrived at French Frigate Shoals, but there they saw two American vessels. They sent messages to Admiral Goto, commander of the Twenty-fourth Air Flotilla at Kwajalein, who ordered a 24-hour postponement in the mission, in the hope that the American ships would go away. But the next day the Japanese submarines spotted two American flying boats near the shoals, and the Japanese concluded that the Americans were using French Frigate Shoals as a seaplane base and there was no room for them to carry out their operation.

The failure of this intelligence operation was a big disappointment to Admiral Yamamoto, who had expected to have the information about the American fleet in Pearl Harbor. But he had made another plan to get that information. A string of submarines had been sent out ahead to lie between Pearl Harbor and Midway, and warn the Japanese as soon as the American fleet left Hawaiian waters.

Yamamoto did not know it, but the Americans, in possession of the information about the coming of the Japanese, had already left Hawaiian waters and were moving on a collision course to intercept the Japanese fleet. So the surprise that Yamamoto had planned had already backfired.

The problem with the whole operation, as the conservatives at the Japanese navy department had said in the beginning, was that it was a response to Admiral Yamamoto's nervous timetable of events. At the outset of the war, he had predicted that he could run the Westerners ragged for six months or so, but after that the Americans would begin to rebound, and with their immense productive capacity, would soon become far too powerful to be defeated. June 1942 was just six months since the attack on Pearl Harbor.

CHAPTER SIX

Nagumo Prepares

On June 1 Admiral Yamamoto assumed, based on a number of events of the day, that the Americans had discovered the coming of the Japanese attack force into the waters of the Eastern Pacific. The main force, in which the flagship *Yamato* was riding, was scheduled to fuel that day with its tankers. But the tankers were not where they were supposed to be, and so on that morning the carrier *Hosho* launched planes to search for the tankers. The search was not successful because of the bad weather, but at this point the tanker leader broke radio silence to let the *Yamato* know where the tankers were located.

After this event Admiral Yamamoto believed that the element of surprise had been lost and the Americans knew where the main force was located. All day long the Japanese intercepted messages from Hawaii and most of them were "urgent" which indicated unusual excitement on the part of the Americans. Five hundred miles northeast of the Japanese-held atoll of Wotje a patrol plane intercepted an American flying boat and they exchanged gunfire, although neither was damaged. But this was another indication of the extension of the American patrol activity, far outside the usual Midway perimeter. American submarines were sighted northeast of Wake Island, another indication of an American effort around Midway.

It was true, the American flying boat had spotted the Japanese main force 700 miles from Midway.

There were some worries among the Yamamoto staff. The submarines of Squadron Five, which were to set up a cordon on June 2, failed to reach their positions, so they could not report on the movement of the American fleet as Yamamoto had expected them to do. Yamamoto had no real idea as to where the Americans were or where they were heading.

What little information Yamamoto did have came from the submarine *I-168*, which was reconnoitering the area. She reported that the Americans were flying off many planes heading southwest, and that many construction cranes were on the island, which meant that some building was in progress.

On June 2, the Nagumo striking force moved into thick fog. That did not help radio reception, and the *Akagi*'s reception was none too good at best. The Nagumo was out of touch with the flagship due to the interdiction against the use of radio, but she would have been out of touch anyhow because of poor reception. Thus Admiral Nagumo did not share Admiral Yamamoto's suspicion that the Japanese forces had been "snooped" by the Americans. He hoped that he still had the element of surprise, and Admiral Yamamoto, not quite sure that he was right, did not break radio silence to tell Nagumo his own fears.

Dawn, June 3. The Nagumo force was still traveling through thick fog. The ships assumed a fog formation, 600 yards apart, with powerful searchlights turned on, but these were scarcely visible to the next ship in the fog. The zigzagging made it dangerous but there was no recourse; they were moving into enemy waters and they had to expect that submarines would be about. Here the Japanese were extremely conscious of their own lack of radar and the American possession of that important aid. The Japanese fleet was blind at the moment, unable to launch antisubmarine patrols because of the fog.

Admiral Nagumo and his staff stood on the admiral's bridge aboard the *Akagi* and stared into the gloomy fog. That day, in order to reach a launch point off Midway to attack that island, the striking force had to change course. There was no way Admiral Nagumo could give visual signals to his other ships, so he had to employ radio. That meant the radio silence was broken, and they had to assume the enemy would know their position and their intentions.

Nagumo had two tasks. First he was to attack Midway Island

and its defenses, softening them up for the landing. Second, he was to strike the enemy fleet and wipe it out if it showed up. But the first task came first, and this was scheduled for June 5.

The problem that bothered Admiral Nagumo was that he did not know where the American fleet was. Could it still be at Pearl Harbor? Could it be in the South Pacific where it had been reported? Could it be just around the horizon, under a cloudy sky? He simply did not know.

His senior staff captain, Captain Oishi, suggested that if the Americans had left Pearl Harbor in response to a broken-code message, they could not have gotten very far, so they could assume that the waters around Midway were clear of American ships and go ahead with the attack on the island.

Rear Admiral Kusaka, the chief of staff of the striking force, suggested that they send low-powered inter-fleet radio messages to the other ships, thus minimizing the danger that the Americans might pick up the transmission. Since something had to be done, Nagumo accepted the suggestion. Usually such messages had a very minimal range, but in this strange weather, when the message was sent, it was picked up by the flagship *Yamato*, 600 miles away!

But the Japanese of the striking force remained supremely confident that they had not been detected and that the Americans were nowhere about. This confidence radiated from within; so often had the striking force been successful in its efforts that it was impossible for Admiral Nagumo and his staff to believe that they would not be successful this time.

Nagumo fretted on his bridge because the weather continued foul and no planes could be flown off for search. The pilots sat in their ready rooms and waited, playing cards or reading. There was nothing to do but wait.

Six hundred miles behind, Admiral Yamamoto's staff was certain that the Americans had been warned, but was also certain that Admiral Nagumo had heard the same transmissions that the Combined Fleet had caught. Therefore, radio silence was maintained, and Admiral Nagumo remained blissfully unaware that the Americans were out and hunting for him. This feeling was reinforced by a message sent out from Imperial General Headquarters in Tokyo, again referring to enemy fleet activity in the Solomon Islands area. The American radio reception down there was working admirably.

The Japanese radio unit in Tokyo also intercepted a number of messages from Pearl Harbor, but so strong was the "Victory disease" that the intelligence officers simply disregarded the Pearl Harbor messages and stuck with their own estimate that the American fleet was operating in the South Pacific.

On June 3 the bad weather which had shrouded the main force finally broke, although the sky was gray and dark all day. At eight o'clock in the morning, Admiral Yamamoto issued orders to Vice Admiral Shiro Takasu's Aleutians guard force to leave the main force and cover the Aleutians operations, so four battleships, two cruisers, and 12 destroyers turned away and headed northeast.

An hour went by, and then Rear Admiral Raizo Tanaka, whose cruisers and destroyers were escorting the 12 transports and three patrol boats that were carrying the Midway invasion troops, reported that his ships had been overflown by an American airplane.

Four hours later, a flight of nine B-17 bombers from Midway Island appeared over the transport force and dropped bombs. But the bombs were delivered from very high altitude and the ships below had no difficulty in maneuvering to avoid them all. But early the next morning the transport convoy was attacked by American torpedo bombers, and one torpedo hit the tanker *Akebono Maru,* damaging her bow and killing several men, but the ship was not seriously hurt and was able to maintain her position in the column.

Now the Combined Fleet staff began for the first time in the operation to worry about the future. They had anticipated that the transports might be discovered, and they had suggested that the striking force go ahead one full day to neutralize the Midway air and shore installations before the transports came up, but Admiral Nagumo had rejected that plan, and suggested instead that the transports delay for a day. But that was impossible because the transports had to conduct an amphibious landing and the tides would not be right except on this one day. So in the argument the cognition of danger was lost, and the original plan was followed. Now it could be seen that the plan was a mistake, but there was nothing that could be done about it.

So the forces forged onward. Meanwhile, the Second Carrier Striking Force, led by Rear Admiral Kakuta against the Alaskan area, was getting under way. The first strike was scheduled for the early hours of June 3, and since sunrise in the summer was very early, 2:58 in the morning, the aircrews and handlers were ready just after 2:00 A.M.

It was cold here in the north—about 20 degrees Fahrenheit—and ships crews were bundled up as they worked the decks. Captain Tadao Kato, the captain of the carrier *Ryujo*, was dressed in a heavy fur coat and on his bridge. He wanted to get going, and suggested to his air officer, Lieutenant Commander Masatake Okumiya, that it was time. But the expected early morning light had not materialized and the decks were still dark, so Okumiya pleaded for more time. Still it did not lighten, and finally staff officers ascertained that they were beset by thick fog that hid the growing daylight.

For this operation the Japanese were singularly badly prepared. The pilots who were to attack Dutch Harbor had maps copied from a chart 30 years old. They had a single photograph of the area, also a quarter of a century old, which showed much of the place as unsurveyed, although it had since been developed. It seemed debatable if the pilots would be able to find the target.

At 2:38 from the bridge of the *Ryujo* they could make out the shapes of other ships and the admiral grew even more restless. He wanted to get the operation into movement, but his staff members were concerned about the safety of the pilots and continued to delay. Five minutes later the light increased and they could see the carrier *Junyo* a half mile away, so the air officer gave the order. Planes began to rise from the flight decks, 23 bombers and 12 fighters, under command of Lieutenant Yoshijo Shiga. The ceiling was so low, 500 feet, that there was no way the planes could circle and form up, so independently they headed for Dutch Harbor, 180 miles to the northeast of the fleet. One bomber crashed into the sea on takeoff but the crew was rescued from the cold waters.

Within minutes after the attack had been launched, the fleet was disturbed by an American flying boat, which circled and then dropped bombs, but did not hit anything.

The planes from the *Ryujo* reached Dutch Harbor at four o'clock and at 4:07 attacked. They bombed a radio station and the oil tanks, and fighters strafed a flying boat moored in the harbor. One fighter was lost on the mission when it was damaged by antiaircraft fire, and made a crash landing on Atka Island, 20 miles northeast of Dutch Harbor. But the pilot broke his neck in the landing and died.

On the way to Dutch Harbor the planes of the *Junyo* met an American flying boat, which they chased and shot down, but in so doing they got lost, so the *Junyo* group did not attack the target at all.

The *Ryujo* planes had another piece of luck. On their return to the carrier they reported on five enemy destroyers lying at Makushin Bay, on the coast of Unalaska Island. Admiral Kakuta ordered an air attack on these ships, and 24 planes headed that way. But the weather closed in around them, and they did not even see the targets, so they returned to the carriers, and the attack force recovered planes and headed toward Midway until it reached a point 1,100 miles offshore.

Four reconnaissance planes from the cruisers *Takao* and *Maya* also went aloft, to try to find the enemy ships, but they had no more success than the carrier planes. They were intercepted by American fighters, which shot down two of the recon planes and damaged the others, so that when they came back to land near their cruisers, both planes broke up when they hit the water.

So the day's operations ended without signal success. The Japanese knew that the Americans had ships and air bases in this area, but that was all they knew. They had not been able to spot any activity at all in the terrible weather.

The Japanese submarines, which were supposed to put a cordon between Hawaii and Midway so they could report when the American fleet sailed out of Pearl Harbor, arrived on station on June 3, long after the Americans had passed by on their way to Midway. But of course the Japanese submarine skippers did not know this, so they patrolled eagerly and carefully and saw nothing. Each submarine remained submerged all day long, and then surfaced at night and watched all the night long for activity from Pearl Harbor. All they saw were flying fish, an occasional marlin breaking the surface, and porpoises playing along.

On the afternoon of June 3, the Nagumo striking force was surging toward Midway at 24 knots, cruising in a defensive ring formation, with four carriers in the center. Earlier there had been some questions raised about the advisability of keeping the carriers so close together, but Nagumo was supremely confident in the ability of the striking force to overcome all enemies. So the carriers were in the center, and the battleships *Haruna* and *Kirishima* and the heavy cruisers *Tone* and *Chikuma* were on the edge, with the light cruiser *Nagara* and 12 destroyers on the outer perimeter. At 1:40 P.M. the cruiser *Tone* suddenly made a signal, reporting the enemy planes sighted, but when three fighter planes from the *Akagi* took off, they found nothing and there was no attack. So Admiral Nagumo deduced that someone aboard the *Tone* was trigger-happy and that there was no threat.

All was quiet in the striking force that night, as the ships steamed steadily toward their objective. At 2:30 on the morning of June 4 there was another alarm. One of the *Akagi* lookouts reported a light off the starboard beam, and said he thought it was an enemy plane. Every man on the bridge strained to see the plane, but it did not appear. Captain Aoki ordered the ship to general quarters and every man went to his action station. Half a minute went by. Nothing. The captain called the lookout. Did he still see the light?

"No, sir," said the chagrined lookout. "I have lost it."

The captain was a little nervous. He had been on his bridge since May 21, the day they left their homeland, living in his sea cabin, without once going to his quarters. He cautioned all the lookouts against making premature reports, but he did not scold them too hard because he did not want to frighten them out of reporting what they saw. But he hoped they would not report any more stars.

He was about to order the ship secured from general quarters when that same lookout piped up:

"Light sighted on starboard beam, bearing 070 degrees. It is not a star, sir."

Captain Aoki ordered a warning flashed to all ships of the striking force. But once more, no one else could see the aircraft, and it never came close.

It was nearing 2:45 A.M., time to launch the attack force that would bomb and strafe Midway installations in preparation for the landing of the troops. The loudspeakers aboard the carriers started squawking, and the aircrews began filtering up to the flight deck to man their planes. The aircraft handlers were finishing the loading of machine guns, and were moving the planes into position. Motors were started and engines roared and began to warm up.

Commander Minoru Genda, the staff operations officer, came up on the bridge. He had been sick with what seemed to be pneumonia almost since leaving Japan, but he got out of his bed to see the launch. Genda had been at the heart of the planning, as he was in the Pearl Harbor and Darwin and Trincomalee strikes. He did not want to miss this one. Sick as he was, he was on the bridge again, with Admiral Nagumo.

Admiral Nagumo was now ready for action. He and his chief of staff made an estimate of the situation at that moment, and found it satisfactory. Their conclusions amounted to this:

1. The American fleet would probably come out and seek battle as soon as Midway landing operations began.

2. Enemy air patrols from Midway would be heavier to the west and to the south, lighter to the north and northwest.

3. The radius of enemy air patrols would be about 500 miles.

4. The enemy had not yet discovered the Japanese battle plan, and he had not yet detected the striking force.

5. There was no evidence of any enemy carriers in the area.

6. The next step was to attack Midway in support of the landings, and destroy the planes and installations there. If the enemy appeared, the striking force could then meet and destroy the enemy carriers.

7. The Americans were expected to offer resistance from land-based aircraft, but the combat air patrol of the carrier force should be able to drive off the enemy planes.

After the sighting of the main force and the abortive bombing, at Pearl Harbor the tension increased steadily. That night Admiral Nimitz wrote in his war diary:

The situation is developing as expected. Carriers, our most important objective, should soon be located. Tomorrow may be the day we can give them the works. The whole course of the war in the Pacific may hinge on the developments of the next two or three days.

That night of June 3 the whole American defense establishment in Hawaii and on the West Coast stood alert. The radio stations on the West Coast closed down early to prevent Japanese bombers from homing in on their signals. Since Admiral King half-expected a raid on the West Coast, a huge fleet of relinquished pleasure craft, manned by naval reserve personnel, put out to sea from every port to patrol the offshore waters and give early warning if the Japanese attempted a landing.

And so the night passed. The Midway atoll was the point of a V, with the two carrier fleets heading toward it, to make the sides of the V. The Japanese carriers were on the northwest, and 400 miles away to the northeast were the American carriers. And each hour the two forces drew closer to one another as they headed south and approached Midway.

CHAPTER SEVEN

Nagumo Attacks

June 4, 3:00 A.M. The men aboard the Japanese carriers were at their action stations. The lights inside the ship were dimmed, and all the watertight doors were dogged down. On the flight deck the planes were noisily warming up, getting ready to launch the attack on Midway's defenses. Aboard the flagship *Akagi*, Commander Mitsuo Fuchida, the air officer, had been ill in sick bay, operated on for appendicitis almost at the moment the ship had left Japan, but he went up on the flight deck to join Commander Masuda, the air officer who was in charge of flight operations.

"When is sunrise?" he asked.

"Five o'clock, sir."

"Have search planes been sent out yet?"

"No. They will go at the same time as the first attack wave."

"Are we using the single-phase search?"

"Yes, sir."

Commander Fuchida did not think much of that. Two months earlier, in the striking force's attacks on Colombo and Trincomalee, the single-phase search system had not served the force very well. Enemy forces had not been spotted until the attack groups were out on their strike missions, and the carriers were at their most vulnerable.

Lieutenant Commander Shigebaru Murata, the commander of the torpedo bomber squadron, told Fuchida not to worry because, after the first wave departed the ship, the second wave, consisting of dive-bombers, torpedo bombers, and Zero fighters, would be available to attack the enemy fleet if it showed up.

As Fuchida knew very well, the searching was all-important this day. They must find the enemy before he found them; it was as simple as that. To do so, the Japanese would employ seven aircraft, one each from *Akagi* and *Kaga*, two each from the cruisers *Tone* and *Chikuma*, and one from the cruiser *Haruna*. Fuchida pondered and still did not like it. A double search pattern would have been much better. He could sense that neither Nagumo or anyone else expected the search to discover anything, for they were certain that the American fleet was nowhere in the area; this single search pattern was perfunctory, designed to prove that point.

If they had really thought the Americans were about they could not have enough search planes out to find them. A double search pattern would have employed 14 planes, two sets flying the same pattern but with a time interval between them. The first set of planes would fly out in darkness and would see nothing on the outward leg, but the second set, starting later, would observe that same area. This was the best the Japanese could do since they did not have radar, as did the Americans. But their planes had longer range than the Americans. Still, by running a single pattern, the Japanese were sacrificing the advantage of their longer range.

Admiral Nagumo had obviously concluded that the American appearance, if at all, would be much later, and that he should get on with his second mission, which was to soften up Midway for the landings. Fuchida found his commander lacking in this regard; he did not know it but Nagumo's reluctance to carry out proper search had cost them a major victory at Trincomalee. The British had three carriers in that area at the time, two of them using a secret island anchorage, but they were out, and if the Japanese had found them they might have made a clean sweep. As it was, they sank the old carrier *Hermes* but missed the chance at the other two.

Search planes were launched by the *Akagi* and the *Kaga* at 4:30 when the first attack wave set out for Midway; at the same time the *Haruna* search plane also set out, but it had a range of only 150 miles because it was an old-type reconnaissance seaplane. The more modern long-range seaplanes from the *Tone* and the *Chikuma* did not get into the air so rapidly. They were half an hour behind schedule. And when the *Chikuma* plane did get up, soon it had to turn back because of a bad engine. So although the search pattern was set for a fan search with seven rays extending out 300 miles, actually one ray was totally uncovered and another was only half-covered. The *Chikuma* plane's search area was where the American fleet actually lay, but the plane never made it far enough out to see the ships.

Commander Fuchida was uneasy. He felt that his navy placed too much emphasis on attack, and not enough on preparations to attack, and that this search was typical of the main problem. In the attack on Pearl Harbor all carrier planes were devoted to the attack, and only the float planes of the cruisers and battleships had been used for observation. Because of this failure, Admiral Nagumo had not realized that there was a great deal left undone at Pearl Harbor; had a proper search been conducted, the planes might well have found Admiral Halsey's carrier *Enterprise,* whose planes had begun to land in Hawaii about the time of the Japanese attack, the carrier was so close.

So the Japanese attack wave took off at a point 240 miles northwest of Midway. It was still 40 minutes until sunrise when the pilots were told to man their planes, and engines were started up again, and the carriers headed into the wind to launch. A Zero fighter was the first off the deck of the *Akagi* and as she winged up, the ship's crew joined in a great cheer for the attackers. Soon the dive-bombers and level bombers were in the air, with their fighter cover, and heading for Midway. In 15 minutes the four carriers launched 108 planes. They circled over the fleet, moved into formation, and headed out southeast. It was 4:45.

The commander of the attack was Lieutenant Joichi Tomonaga, leading 36 type-97 level bombers from the *Soryu* and the *Hiryu*. Off to their left were the 36 dive-bombers from the

Akagi and the *Kaga*. And flying cover were 36 Zero fighters, nine from each of the four carriers.

These were all experienced pilots, the first string of the Japanese naval air force. Lieutenant Tomonaga had gained an enormous amount of experience fighting in China since 1937. Lieutenant Suganami, the fighter commander, had also participated in all these battles.

The sound of their engines died out and the carriers steamed on, now preparing for the second wave. This second wave, according to the plan of attack, was armed for an assault on the American fleet, should it be found. The planners had anticipated that the attack on Midway would knock out the defenses and then the Japanese carrier force would be free to move when the American fleet showed up. So the second wave began arming at 5:00 A.M. Each dive-bomber carried a 250-kilogram bomb, and the level bombers each carried a torpedo. Again the force was 108 planes, three waves of 36 fighters, dive-bombers, and torpedo bombers.

This group of fliers was even more highly experienced. The leader of the dive-bombers, Lieutenant Commander Takeshi Egusa, was regarded as the navy's leading expert on dive-bombing tactics, and he had led the attack on the *Hermes* and the cruisers *Dorsetshire* and *Cornwall* which had sunk all three ships off Ceylon a few months earlier. Commander Murata led the torpedo bombers. Here again was an expert. Murata was the man who had devised the plan and helped formulate the torpedo modifications to make the Pearl Harbor attack possible. At first the opponents of the Pearl Harbor attack had said the harbor was too shallow for torpedoes to run in it. But Murata had worked with the torpedo men to revise the standards so that the torpedoes would function in shallow water and the results had been spectacular.

And finally the commander of the fighter contingent for this second strike was Lieutenant Commander Shigeru Itaya, already an ace with more than five victories and much experience in China with the fleet.

Although this was the second strike, it was the first team, for Admiral Nagumo had kept aboard his best men just in case the American fleet showed up—which he now did not expect, based on the faulty intelligence at his command and on his own decision (really Chief of Staff Kusaka's) to run the short-course search plan instead of a thorough one. Another calculated decision by Admiral Nagumo and his staff: they had allocated only 18 fighter planes for combat air patrol, to cover the four carriers and their escorting vessels, so that they could provide maximum fighter coverage for the bombers of the first and second strikes.

When Commander Fuchida had learned this he had been dismayed, but since he was still officially sick and recuperating from his operation, he had not been consulted. Further, as if from afar, Fuchida recognized the essential weakness of the Japanese plan, calling for the dual use of the carriers to support the land operations and to guard against the coming of the American fleet. This problem would not have occurred had the *Zuikaku* and the *Shokaku* been along. Each of those carriers accommodated 60 planes, which would have meant an entire third echelon, so Nagumo could then have easily carried both tasks with no thought of surprise. As it was, he was steaming very close to an atoll with a deckload of aircraft—a primary target for either land-based air attackers or the American carriers if they should suddenly appear. Thus can be seen the extent of the reverberations of the battle of the Coral Sea; just now the American strategic victory there was clear.

Fuchida had been so concerned with the takeoff of the first wave that he had asked about the combat air patrol and been devastated to learn that only nine planes had taken off from the *Akagi* and another nine planes were standing by. Nine planes for four carriers. The Americans usually used five planes per carrier for combat air patrol.

Fuchida at this point had been overcome with weariness and had returned to his cabin below the flight deck. But he had been below for just a few moments when the bugle blew to sound the air raid alarm throughout the ship's communications system. The nine other fighters were now ordered into the air from the *Akagi*. It was 5:20 A.M. Five minutes later the anti-aircraft guns began to fire, and Fuchida went up to the flight deck again to see what was the matter. They told him that an American flying boat had been discovered snooping around the fleet. The PBY had approached through cloud cover, and by the time the Japanese fighters could move toward it, or the new fighters could get into the air, the pilot had taken a good look and ducked back into the clouds. He was nowhere about.

Soon the Japanese radio operators intercepted a long report in coded English emanating from a point near their fleet. They knew what it was: the PBY was making its report, and soon they could expect visitors, but whether from Midway or from American carriers they did not know. They did know, finally, that they had been discovered by the enemy, but they had no idea that the American fleet was only 200 miles northeast of them, well within striking distance.

Then, minutes after the fighters were alerted, one of the cruiser *Tone*'s air search planes, about 40 miles from the carriers, sighted a PBY, whether the same one or another, heading for the Japanese fleet. Seven minutes later, at 5:42, the flying boat became visible from the deck of the flagship and the fighter planes were told to give chase.

For an hour the Japanese combat air patrol played hide-and-seek with a succession of American observation planes. The *Tone*'s search plane reported that 15 enemy aircraft were heading toward the Japanese striking force. The commander ordered the speed raised to 28 knots, and the *Tone* began to make smoke to cover the carriers. They were constantly observed by a succession of PBYs, which moved in and out of the cloud cover, and though the Japanese Zeros gave chase, they never got close enough to fire.

Admiral Nagumo asked if the search planes out there had spotted anything and was told that there was no sign of the American fleet. That was true; the plane given the sector where the Americans could be found was the one that had turned back with engine trouble.

Meanwhile, Lieutenant Tomonaga led the first attack wave against Midway Island. At 4:45 the planes had climbed to 12,000 feet and headed southeast toward the atoll. A hundred and fifty miles out they were spotted by an American flying boat which shadowed them and then when they were 30 miles offshore at Midway, climbed up and dropped a parachute flare.

When the flare went off, the American planes, which were in the air, moved to attack.

Actually the Americans had been waiting since just before six o'clock when the Midway search radar had picked up the blips of the approaching attack force. So the fighters were put up and all the other aircraft, which would be very susceptible on the ground, were ordered to get into the air and get away from the battle.

Just after 6:15 the air battle began. Major Floyd B. Parks's fighter squadron climbed to 17,000 feet, and came down to attack the Japanese bombers, who were flying at 12,000 feet.

The American air defense consisted of 32 PBY patrol bombers, six torpedo bombers of Vt-8, 20 old-fashioned Buffalo fighter planes of Vmf-221, and seven more modern F4F7 fighters; VMSB-241, the marine dive-bomber squadron, had 11 SB2U-3 bombers called Vindicators and 16 SBD bombers. The army air force had four B-16 bombers and 19 B-17s.

Many of the fighter planes were in the air, and others took off from Midway. From 6:45 to 7:10 the American fighter planes challenged the Japanese above the atoll, but the Zero fighter was so far superior to the Buffalo and superior to the F4F7 in speed and performance that the contest was most uneven. Besides, the Japanese fighters outnumbered the Americans; in this regard Admiral Nagumo and his staff had been right: the presence of so many Japanese fighter planes made the task of the Japanese bombers much easier.

Almost every American fighter plane was thrown onto the defensive by the speed and fast turns of the Zeros. But the Americans did their best, and they led the Japanese fighters over the antiaircraft defenses. The Japanese bombers then came in, first the level bombers, which dropped their bombs from 14,000 feet, and then the dive-bombers.

The level bombers carried bombs of about 1,800 pounds and the dive-bombers carried 500-pound bombs. Bombs destroyed the marine command post of defense for the island,

and demolished the mess hall and damaged the powerhouse on Eastern Island and burned the oil tanks on nearby Sand Island. They also set storehouses and the hospital afire, and wrecked the seaplane hangar. But they did not knock out the antiaircraft guns, which they characterized as rendering vicious fire, and they failed to destroy the runways. Surveying the damage and their losses, Lieutenant Tomonaga had to decide what to recommend to Admiral Nagumo. The fighters had done an excellent job of protecting the bombers; not one American fighter had shot down a Japanese plane, but one fighter and three bombers were shot down by antiaircraft fire. Obviously there was plenty of fight left in those Americans, so Lieutenant Tomonaga knew what was wanted. The primary objective of the strike was to destroy American air power at Midway. To be sure, they had shot down most of the fighters—17 of the 26—but all the bombers and the amphibious and seaplanes had escaped. At 7:00 A.M. Tomonaga made the decision. As he led the strike force back toward the carriers, he recommended another air strike on Midway that morning.

On Midway, charged up by the battle, the defenders overestimated the fighter force that had attacked them, but only by about a dozen, and correctly estimated the number of bombers (72). But the fighting had been so swift and so vigorous and there had been so much shooting from the ground that the defenders thought they had shot down 53 planes, when actually only six Japanese planes failed to return to the carriers. But the Japanese also exaggerated, or made error, and they came back with tales of shooting down 42 American fighters, instead of 17. But the Japanese had done harm to the enemy: only two of the American fighters were undamaged.

Back aboard the Japanese carriers, while the air strike was in progress, Admiral Nagumo and his men faced an American attack by bombers from Midway. Admiral Nimitz had told the chief of the American defense force on Midway to do everything possible to damage the Japanese carriers as soon as they could be found. So the six new TBF torpedo bombers, which had recently arrived at Midway, and the four army B-26 medium bombers were armed with torpedoes and sent out. They arrived over the carriers at 7:10, but they were not very successful. Four planes were shot down before they could launch, and when the planes did launch the torpedoes seemed to the Japanese to be very slow, so slow in fact that one was destroyed in the water by strafing. One American torpedo plane, hit by antiaircraft fire, crashed onto the flight deck of the *Akagi* and then bounced into the sea. Three more were shot down by the ship's antiaircraft guns.

Here is the account from Mitsuo Fuchida and Masatake Okumiya's *Midway*. Since Fuchida saw it all, he had the eye-witness sense of the battle:

> Following the lead of the destroyers, our cruisers opened fire. Then battleship *Kirishima*, to starboard of *Akagi*, loosed her main batteries at the attackers. Still they kept coming in, flying low over the water. Black bursts of antiaircraft fire blossomed all around them, but one of the raiders went down. As *Akagi*'s guns commenced firing, three Zeros braved their own antiaircraft barrage and dove down on the Americans. In a moment's time, three of the enemy were set aflame and splashed into the water, raising tall columns of smoke. . . . About this time several torpedoes passed to port of *Akagi*, trailing pale white wakes. *Akagi* had maneuvered so skillfully that not one torpedo scored and everyone breathed a deep sigh of relief.

Only two army B-26 bombers returned. The pilots again exaggerated, claiming three hits on the carriers. Actually there was not even a near-miss.

The American attack had failed physically, but it did have an effect on the battle. Admiral Nagumo had received Lieutenant Tomonaga's call for another strike on Midway. True to form, he hesitated. He did not like having his carriers so close to land in enemy territory. But he had seen no sign of an enemy fleet, nor was there any indication from Yamamoto or anyone else of the American awareness of the Japanese presence.

And so Lieutenant Tomonaga's message was approved and the orders were given for a second strike to be made on the island.

CHAPTER EIGHT

Counterattack and Check

In the middle of the attack by the Midway-based planes against the Japanese striking force, Admiral Kusaka had word from the cruiser *Tone*. Her search plane had been launched half an hour late, and had moved out on a course of 100 degrees to a limit of 300 miles. The plane then turned north and flew for 60 miles and then headed back to the carrier. Two hundred miles from the Japanese force, the pilot spotted a formation of ships, and identified them as warships, although the first message said nothing about type.

This was at 7:28. The message was delayed in transit from the pilot to the *Tone* to the flagship, and did not reach Admiral Nagumo until he was in the middle of the American attack.

Admiral Kusaka was mildly annoyed at the *Tone* plane report. Not very illuminating, he said. What sort of ships were they? If they were battleships and cruisers they were still a long way off. But if they included aircraft carriers, that meant the striking force was now within the range of the enemy. An order was sent to the pilot to describe the ships he had seen.

Until now, there had not been the slightest indication that the American fleet existed anywhere near Midway; the Japanese still thought the carriers might be in the South Pacific, an opinion strengthened by transmissions from Tokyo. Therefore when Admiral Nagumo decided on the basis of the attacks by the Midway-based planes that Midway did indeed need another working-over by the bombers and fighters, no one worried about the fact that the American fleet was within 200 miles.

The torpedoes had already been racked up on the level bombers aboard the *Akagi* and *Kaga* and they had to be disarmed and removed, replaced by high-explosive bombs. The dive-bombers had been loaded with armor-piercing shells for a fight against ships; these, too, had to be removed and high-explosive bombs substituted. So the plane handlers went to work.

The same was happening aboard the *Hiryu* and *Soryu*, when they were suddenly attacked by 14 B-17 bombers. Splashes could be seen all around both ships, but neither was hit; the bombing was carried out from too high a level and the ship handlers had plenty of time to turn out of the way. The bombers returned to Midway to report four hits on the carriers, but it was not true. There was one. But by the same token, the bombers returned unscathed. The altitude was too high for the Japanese antiaircraft gunners, and the fighters were not ordered to attack the big planes, because they had a fearsome reputation.

Admiral Nagumo was concerned about more attacks from Midway, and so he ordered the 36 fighters of the second wave to take off and join the combat air patrol.

This action was justified a few minutes later when 16 Marine Corps dive-bombers attacked. The bomber pilots were totally inexperienced in this type of plane and because of a fuel shortage on Midway they had not been able to get the experience they needed, so their commander, Major Lofton Henderson, decided to make a glide bombing attack instead of dive-bombing. It was an error because the Sbd was very slow, and the Zero was very fast. Consequently, those 40-odd Zeros above pounced on the bombers and shot down eight of them. Six others managed to limp back to Midway where they either crash-landed, or were junked. Only two planes survived the attack, and one of them even managed to strafe the carrier *Hiryu*, killing four Japanese sailors. Then came 11 more marine bombers to attack the carriers. But so great was the antiaircraft fire and so tenacious the Zeros that the flight leader shifted the target to the battleship *Haruna*, and dropped bombs, but all the bombs missed. Nine of those planes managed to make it back to Midway.

Meanwhile Admiral Nagumo had another worry. The American submarine *Nautilus* was in the area. Destroyers had made contact and depth-charged her early that morning, but she had escaped and now came up to periscope depth in the middle of the Japanese attack force formation. She fired one torpedo at a battleship at a range of three miles, and missed, and then had to dive deep to escape another depth-charging.

By 8:30 things had quieted down around the carriers. The last of the American planes had turned back to Midway, and the submarine was down deep. At this point the Japanese planes of the first air strike against Midway were moving in toward the carriers, and the flight decks had to be cleared to handle them.

Aboard the *Akagi*, Admiral Nagumo and his staff assessed their situation with considerable confidence. From what they had seen this morning, they did not appear to have much to fear from the Americans, no matter how many planes they sent; the levels of American experience and skill so far shown were very low by Japanese standards.

So when a destroyer on the perimeter of the formation signaled that it had spotted about a hundred enemy planes coming in, Nagumo was ready. But it was not even an attack, as it turned out, but the first strike returning at 8:30. So the plane recovery began. There was a little confusion because the Japanese carriers had dispersed over a wide area in their maneuvering to avoid the American attacks, but this was steadily lessened and the ships began to prepare to return to their tight defensive formation. The carriers turned into the wind as the handlers cleared the decks, and at 8:37 the flagship signaled "commence landing" and the first strike planes began coming back aboard their carriers.

Twenty-three minutes later the last carrier reported all planes recovered. Admiral Nagumo then waited for reports to assess the success of the attack. Three of the returning planes had been badly shot up, but they managed to land safely, although the pilot of one plane, wounded, passed out the minute his plane was seized by the restraining wire.

* * *

In the midst of the landing operations, the ship's plane handlers also had orders to stop the rearming of the second strike bombers with high explosives. The electrifying news that enemy ships had been sighted meant—whether they were carriers or not—that the second strike would be sent against enemy ships. So Admiral Nagumo told the crews to keep any torpedoes that had not yet been removed. Consequently, the carrier planes were made ready with a mixture of armament.

That first demand by Admiral Nagumo for identification of the ships in question was not answered in the next message from the *Tone* pilot, who told of course change by the apparently enemy ships.

In reply to the second message, the pilot said: "Five cruisers and five destroyers."

The tranquility of the flagship bridge was restored. The intelligence officer said he had known it all the time. Admiral Kusaka, the chief of staff, said it was not a problem, they could take care of the enemy ships later with a strike or two. So he advised Nagumo to make the second strike against Midway, which would mean adjusting more of the planes again.

This was under consideration 10 minutes later, when the *Tone* again sent a message from her pilot. There appeared to be an aircraft carrier with the five cruisers and five destroyers, said the message.

This was confusing. If there was a carrier, why had the carrier not joined in the land-based attack on the Japanese ships by sending its planes?

Was there a carrier there or not? That *Tone* pilot certainly did not give much information. A few minutes later came another message from the *Tone* pilot. Now he said he saw two more cruisers joining that force.

Admiral Kusaka then decided that there must be at least one carrier in that group of ships. Admiral Nagumo agreed that they must make that presumption, even without information, and the strike on the naval force must take precedence over the second attack on Midway.

But when could they launch their second attack? All 36 fighters scheduled for that wave were already in the air, and had been for half an hour. The torpedo planes were in the process of armament, disarmament, armament. So the only planes ready were the 36 dive-bombers of the *Hiryu* and the *Soryu*. But it was contrary to Japanese naval doctrine to send bombers without a fighter escort.

What to do about the torpedo planes, half with one sort of armament, half with another? Nagumo pondered.

Rear Admiral Tamon Yamaguchi, the commander of Carrier Division Two (the *Hiryu* and the *Soryu*), advocated an immediate attack with whatever was ready. But Nagumo was a more cautious man, and he opted to recover his fighters in the air, re-gas and rearm them, and then send off the second strike against the American fleet.

While he was doing this, Nagumo began to retire to the north, to put some distance between himself and the American fleet, expecting to later turn around and destroy the enemy force. And this was to be done in an orderly fashion. All the torpedo bombers on the decks were ordered below to rearm with torpedoes, not bombs, and the plane handlers began moving them.

Although air officer Masuda joked about the quick changes, the work below on the hangar deck was pursued furiously. The plane handlers removed the 800-kilogram bombs and stacked them on the deck; there was no time to trundle them down to the magazine where they should have gone for safety's sake.

At 8:55 Admiral Nagumo sent the order to the force to move northward and make preparations to send the strike against the enemy ships.

Admiral Nagumo also sent a message to Admiral Yamamoto informing him of the discovery of a carrier and 10 other warships and of his intention to fight them. A copy went to Vice Admiral Kondo, commander of the Midway invasion force, so he would know the second strike against Midway had not been launched.

By 9:18 the last of the fighter planes had been recovered and the Japanese fleet was speeding northward, thus to avoid the land-based air attack from the Midway air force, and also to get into a position to attack the American carrier, if it was one. No one was really certain about that, even yet.

And because no one was certain, the character and training and inclinations of Admiral Nagumo controlled the situation. And in that hour of decision the admiral, wondering what to do about the American fleet, betrayed his innate conservatism and lack of confidence in his carrier weapons, and made a decision that ultimately cost him the battle.

But no one knew these facts at that moment. All they knew was that the Nagumo force was moving north, away from the enemy, while the plane handlers worked feverishly to prepare the aircraft for attack on ships. The 36 dive-bombers from the *Hiryu* and the *Soryu* and 54 torpedo bombers would be used, which included some f ɔm the first strike—18 bombers each from the *Akagi* and the *Kaga* and nine each from the *Hiryu* and the *Soryu*. Now, however, only 12 Zero fighters could be used to escort the bombers. So why had not Admiral Nagumo sent the bombers off alone? Simply because Japanese carrier doctrine was structured so that bombers must have fighter protection even if that protection was not enough to protect. Thus are wars lost, by adherence to pieces of paper in time of trial.

CHAPTER NINE

The Americans Move

It was the night before the battle. Lieutenant Commander John C. Waldron, the commanding officer of Torpedo Eight, as they called the Hornet's *torpedo squadron, was preparing his battle plan for that moment when they found the Japanese aircraft carriers. He sketched out his program, the order of fight and the order of attack. And as he did so, he thought about the action they faced, probably the next day, June 4. No one was more aware than Lieutenant Commander Waldron of the deficiencies of the TBD torpedo bombers. They were cumbersome, slow, and short of range. They carried a radio operator who was also a gunner, but with their small machine guns they were no match in any way for the Japanese Zero fighters that would come up to oppose them, and Commander Waldron wondered that night how many of his airmen would survive the attack to be made:*

"I feel we are all ready. I actually believe that under these conditions we are the best in the world. My greatest hope is that we encounter a favorable tactical situation, but if we don't, and the worst comes to the worst, I want each of us to do the utmost to destroy his enemies. If there is only one plane left to make a final run-in, I want that man to go in and get a hit. May God be with us all . . ."

Rear Admiral Raymond Spruance, on Admiral Halsey's recommendation, had taken command of the task force that included the carriers *Enterprise* and *Hornet*, when Halsey had to go into the hospital. They had left Pearl Harbor on May 28, long before the arrival off the islands of the Japanese submarines. In fact, American submarines had gone out even earlier in May, a dozen of them, to patrol off Midway and watch for the Japanese fleet, while seven more patrolled halfway between Midway and Hawaii.

By May 29 the *Yorktown* was repaired as well as she could be on such short notice, and ready for sea she sailed the next day to conduct some training exercises and then join Admiral Spruance in the search for the Japanese fleet.

On May 31 the three carriers and their supporting ships met at sea with two oilers and refueled. On June 2 the entire American force assembled about 325 miles northeast of Midway. The Americans had three carriers, eight cruisers, and 15 destroyers, plus two more destroyers, guarding the two tankers. The three carriers altogether had 243 planes. The four Japanese carriers had 273 planes; the support warship force consisted of two heavy cruisers and one light cruiser, two battleships, and 12 destroyers.

As of June 1, the American ships were far out to sea, beyond the capability of the American land-based air forces to support them, so that day they mounted combat air patrols and flew search missions.

The Americans had the great advantage of knowing exactly what they were doing and what the enemy had planned. On June 2 more search missions were flown, but the weather was so bad the last missions had to be canceled and nothing was found. That day Admiral Spruance sent a message to all the ships under his command, telling them that the Japanese were mounting an assault on Midway, and that they could expect to meet four or five carriers. He assured them that the American presence was unknown to the enemy, and that they had a chance to inflict serious damage on the Japanese. But first they had to find the enemy.

On the morning of June 3, Ensign Jack Reid of the Midway patrol wing detachment found the Japanese for them, but it was not the carrier force: it was the seaplane carriers and the transports loaded with troops who were to occupy the two Midway atoll islands.

At Midway, Captain Cyril Simard immediately dispatched nine army B-17 bombers to attack this force and late in the afternoon they attacked without result, although the army pilots claimed hits on two warships. That night four PBY flying boats carrying torpedoes also attacked, led to the enemy by radar, and one torpedo hit and damaged the *Akebono Maru,* as noted, but not seriously enough to stop her.

When that news reached Pearl Harbor Nimitz knew the battle had begun. The problem now was to find the Japanese, to surprise them and attack the carriers, before the Japanese could find the American fleet.

That night of June 3 when Spruance learned that the land-based planes had attacked a part of the Japanese force, but no carriers, the Americans were 300 miles northeast of Midway.

Although Admiral Spruance was in command of the two-carrier task force, he was not the overall commander of the operation; under American naval practice the senior admiral was in command, and Vice Admiral Frank Jack Fletcher was senior to Rear Admiral Spruance. So the overall command was in the hands of Fletcher and he received the communications from Midway and the Pacific Fleet Headquarters at Pearl Harbor. For once Fletcher trusted his radio intelligence reports, which said that a Japanese carrier striking force was approaching Midway from the northwest to launch an attack on the islands at dawn on June 4. Fletcher adjusted the course of the American fleet, heading southwest, so that the Americans would arrive about 200 miles north of Midway at dawn, when they would attack just as soon as they found the Japanese carriers.

First light began on the morning of June 4 at about 4:00 A.M. and the sun rose at 4:57. It was a fine day, too fine for a carrier commander's comfort, with very light breezes that did not help in the launching and recovery of planes, and an almost cloudless sky that gave good visibility for 40 miles.

At 4:30 that morning, the *Yorktown* launched 10 dive-bombers which flew out to the north covering a half circle. At that moment, Admiral Nagumo was about 200 miles to the west, and the first Japanese air strike against Midway was being launched. As noted, the PBYs operating from Midway found the Japanese carrier force that morning and notified the fleet. The message was brief and to the point: "Enemy carriers," and the location and bearings of the ships. The PBYs kept up a string of messages, tracking the enemy ships and locating them for the American fleet, but mentioned only two of the Japanese carriers.

As usual Admiral Fletcher delayed the attack. He wanted to cover his search planes before sending off a strike. So just after six o'clock that morning he ordered Admiral Spruance to take the *Enterprise* and the *Hornet* southwest and as soon as they could find the enemy carriers, to attack.

As soon as he could recover his planes, he would follow, said Admiral Fletcher. It was hardly an aggressive stance, but Fletcher was notorious for his supercaution.

He and Admiral Nagumo were very much alike; in this case Fletcher's failure to act hurt nothing, because Spruance was there with two carriers to carry the ball, as it were, while Nagumo's failure cost him the initiative.

A little over an hour after the sun rose, Admiral Spruance ordered his task force ships to general quarters and the men hurried to their action stations. Two carriers, six cruisers, and nine destroyers speeded up to 25 knots and headed southwest toward the area where they would find the enemy. The aviators in their ready rooms had been ready for action since shortly after midnight.

Admiral Spruance was very lucky. His experience was totally confined to surface ships and his understanding of carrier tactics was rudimentary. But he had aboard the *Enterprise* that day Captain Miles W. Browning, Halsey's chief of staff and an aviator. Spruance had planned to wait until the task force reached a point about a hundred miles from the Japanese fleet to launch the air strike. But Captain Browning pointed out that they knew the Japanese had sent a strike against Midway, and from the radio reports he could estimate that the strike would be returning to the Japanese carriers just about at nine o'clock, the time Spruance planned to launch his planes. If they would launch two hours earlier, they could arrive over the Japanese fleet just at the time of utmost confusion, when the carriers were involved in recovering planes and preparing to send another strike out.

That posed a very difficult decision for Admiral Spruance who was not by nature a very adventurous man. The big problem was the short range of the American torpedo planes—350 miles. That meant for all practical purposes they must be not more than 175 miles from their target when launched. If they were farther away, some planes would not make it back to the carriers. But Spruance was well aware of the importance of this battle to the American war effort. If it was lost, and the American carriers were sunk, the Pacific Fleet would indeed be crippled, and the Japanese could attack and capture Hawaii without much trouble. The whole Pacific war effort was very definitely at stake.

So Admiral Spruance made the difficult decision, prompted by Captain Browning, and the American planes began taking off from the decks of the *Enterprise* and the *Hornet* just after seven o'clock.

The *Hornet* air group's battle plan called for the dive-bombers and torpedo bombers to travel together, escorted by Wildcat fighter planes. This was always a problem, because the dive-bombers were faster than the lumbering torpedo planes, and it was not unusual for them to get separated, particularly if they encountered weather which would prevent them from keeping visual contact.

That morning Lieutenant Commander Waldron came up to Captain Marc Mitscher for a final briefing. It was not a very happy occasion, because Waldron knew that no matter what happened, his torpedo planes were going to be slaughtered, either by antiaircraft fire as they went in to attack, or by Zero fighters.

And if by some miracle the planes managed to get in to attack and get out again, they still would not have enough fuel to get back to their carrier. The chances of their being found were remote. Commander Waldron did not expect to survive this mission, nor did he expect his men to come back. They were the victims of an ancient technology; their planes had not kept abreast of the times, and while far better torpedo bombers were under manufacture in the United States just then, the old TBD was the only weapon available to them at the moment.

The two carriers then separated, following the carrier doctrine of 1942, which held that carriers should operate at some distance from each other so that if enemy planes came to attack, they would have to make a choice, and one carrier at least might be spared a heavy assault. This was the exact opposite of the Japanese carrier doctrine, which called for the massing of carriers to create a common defense pattern. Thus, while the American carriers moved away from each other, the Japanese carriers remained in constant view of one another.

While the American carriers were launching their planes, the Japanese plane from the cruiser *Tone* was spotted above, so Admiral Spruance knew his task force had been sighted and the enemy would soon be taking some action. Spruance then worried that he had already lost the initiative and the element of surprise. But Captain Browning pointed out that the Japanese still had to recover the planes of that first strike.

Browning also persuaded Spruance to go all-out in the attack; that is, to use every possible aircraft on this strike and hit the enemy as hard as could be done. This created a problem, because half the planes to be used were down on the hangar deck and had to be brought back up on the elevators, and so the launch took over an hour, which meant that many planes were aloft, circling and waiting and using up precious gasoline.

So the strike from the *Enterprise* and the *Hornet* was under way, with 18 Wildcat fighter planes, 67 Douglas Dauntless dive-bombers, and 29 Devastator torpedo bombers. Spruance retained 36 fighters for combat air patrol above the task force, 18 in the air and 18 on the carriers to relieve them.

As soon as the planes were launched, the carriers and their escort ships resumed a course of 240 degrees, heading toward the enemy at 25 knots, eating up the distance between the forces, and giving the planes of the air strike a better chance to hit and then get home again.

There was one other positive factor. The Japanese fleet was close on Midway, and so the American torpedo bombers might land on Eastern Island as an alternative to getting back to the carriers.

Admiral Fletcher adopted the same course, but he delayed the launch of his planes for more than two hours. If the battle had been left to him, it might well have been lost by such tactics. It was nearly nine o'clock before he launched half his dive-bombers and all his torpedo planes.

By this time, the operations room at Pearl Harbor was abuzz with reports from the fleet and reports from Midway. The Midway communiqués featured the exaggerated perceptions of the pilots, who thought they had seriously damaged part of Nagumo's fleet; in reality they had done no damage at all, except to that one tanker with the supply and landing force.

At 8:30 Midway had sobering news: "Only three fighting planes remain." So Midway had shot its wad. One disquieting bit of news was that the Japanese Zeros had made mincemeat of the American torpedo bombers, which were far too slow for their task.

Now the balance rested squarely with the fighting fleet. At Pearl Harbor the tension grew unbearable, and Admiral Nimitz left the operations room and took refuge in his office. His intelligence officer, Commander Edwin T. Layton, went to his own office, and kept in touch by telephone with Commander Rochefort's radio intelligence unit, which was monitoring the Japanese radio and picking up the words of Nagumo's pilots. Thus Layton learned and told Nimitz that the American fleet had been sighted by a Japanese scout plane. But Nimitz also had the comforting news that the planes of the *Hornet* and *Enterprise* were winging toward the Japanese and should catch the Japanese carriers with their decks full of planes.

At 19,000 feet, the American planes made their way toward the Japanese striking force, which steamed steadily onward. The four carriers tightened up their box formation, with the battleships and cruisers and destroyers surrounding them. The flagship *Akagi* was on the starboard side and a mile behind her came the *Kaga*. Carrier Division Two, the *Soryu* and the flagship *Hiryu*, were steaming two miles to the port of the first division.

The Japanese carriers had begun recovering the planes of the first strike shortly after 8:00 A.M. that morning. A few minutes later, Admiral Nagumo had warning about the approach of enemy carrier planes, so he changed course to the northeast even before all the planes were recovered. By this course change, the Japanese moved out of the path of the *Hornet*'s 35 dive-bombers, and when they arrived where they thought the Japanese should be and found nothing, they headed toward Midway hoping to find the enemy, and by this took themselves completely out of the battle. Thirteen bombers landed at Midway, two crash-landed in the lagoon, and all the fighters were forced into the sea when they ran out of gas.

So now it was up to the *Hornet* torpedo planes.

On the way to the Japanese fleet, as was half-expected the *Hornet* torpedo bombers, which were traveling down "on the deck," got separated from the high-flying dive-bombers when they ran into cloud layers. Then, when the Japanese carriers did not turn out to be where the sighting reports had indicated, Lieutenant Commander Waldron made the right decision and turned north, while the dive-bombers headed toward Midway. Just before 9:30 Waldron saw two columns of smoke on the horizon. There was the Japanese fleet.

Meanwhile a Zero of the Japanese combat air patrol sent a hurried warning down to the *Akagi*.

Still the bombers could not be seen from the decks of the carriers.

But the idea that torpedo planes were heading toward them was alarming.

Admiral Nagumo and his staff recoiled. The decks of their carriers were at their most vulnerable point possible, their decks filled with planes, gasoline hoses, ammunition trolleys, bombs, and torpedoes. Down below the torpedoes and high-explosive bombs, moved around so much in the past few hours, were stacked on the hangar deck. There was no time to move them into magazines.

Then on the *Akagi*'s starboard bow, the lookouts spotted the tiny dark specks a little above the horizon, and then saw wings flashing in the sun. From above, the Zeros of the combat air patrol saw too, and came flashing down from 15,000 feet to strike the low-flying torpedo bombers. The Japanese were surprised to see that the torpedo planes were without fighter protection. And there were 48 Zeros in the air, with but one idea at the moment.

Waldron headed in to the enemy, but he never had a chance. Half a dozen Zeros were after him before he got within range of the carrier. Antiaircraft fire began to come up from the ships ringing the carriers, and there was still eight miles to go.

In they went into a hail of fire, and one after the other the planes flamed and fell, as the Zeros and the flak got to them. Fifteen planes, 30 men, went into the sea, and there was but one survivor, Ensign George H. Gay, whose plane was shot down just after he launched his torpedo. His radioman was killed, and the plane crashed into the water. Gay managed to struggle to the surface as the plane sank, and hid under a floating seat cushion to avoid the attention of Japanese planes, which came down to strafe the wreckage of the American torpedo bombers. From there he watched what happened next.

The Zero fighter group leader reported to the *Akagi*: "All fifteen enemy torpedo bombers shot down," but hardly had he finished when a lookout aboard the *Akagi* shouted out again:

"Enemy torpedo planes approaching forty degrees port."

This was Torpedo Six, the *Enterprise* torpedo squadron. It, too, was without fighter protection, because the fighters had strayed. Lieutenant Commander Eugene F. Lindsey, the commander of the squadron, saw how low he was on gasoline, and without warning, he bored in to attack. Planes came down on both sides of the Japanese carriers, and on the deck of the *Akagi* Commander Fuchida did not see how they all could possibly fail to make a strike. But once again the Zeros, with their infinitely greater speed and maneuverability, were on the slow bombers, and 10 of the 14 *Enterprise* torpedo planes, including Lieutenant Commander Lindsey's, were shot down. A few planes managed to launch their torpedoes, but from so long a range that it was easy for the Japanese ships to avoid them.

Now it was 10:00 A.M. The *Yorktown*'s Torpedo Thirty-one arrived on the scene escorted by six fighters. But these were soon shot down; Lieutenant Commander Lance E. Massey chose the *Hiryu* as the target, and the planes followed him as he went in after her. Seven of the bombers managed to launch torpedoes, five from the starboard side and two from the port, but the captain of the carrier turned sharply to starboard, and either those port torpedoes missed, or as so often happened with American torpedoes in these early days of the war, they misfired. The *Hiryu* was unhurt.

So the three squadrons of American torpedo bombers had made their attacks, and all had failed. From them all, only four of the *Enterprise* and two of the *Yorktown* torpedo bombers managed to make it back to the carriers. Forty-one planes had attacked, and not one had scored.

All this while the Japanese had been landing and sending off fighters and the preparations for the strike against the American fleet continued as the ship captains maneuvered. Planes were brought up from the hangar deck, ready to fly, and at 10:20 Admiral Nagumo gave the general order to the carriers to launch when ready. On the flight deck of the *Akagi* the strike planes were warming their engines, and the carrier began turning into the wind to launch.

Up above, the broken cloud cover did not seriously impair visibility and the lookouts scanned the horizon and the cloud cover. At 10:24 came the order from the bridge of the *Akagi* to begin launching planes, and the air officer waved a white flag and a Zero went down the deck and took off. Just then a lookout shouted:

"Hell divers."

On the bridge Commander Fuchida looked up. He saw three black shapes dropping like stones out of the cloud cover at 10,000 feet headed for his ship. The antiaircraft gunners manned their guns and began firing. But the Zeros, which had been drawn down low toward the water to shoot down those torpedo bombers, were of no use in stopping the dive-bombers before they went into their dives and then it was impossible.

Commander Fuchida dropped to the deck and crawled for cover.

Then he heard the scream of the bombers heading for the ship; there was the explosion of a bomb, a flash, and another explosion. He was shaken by a blast of hot air, and then everything was quiet aboard the ship.

Fuchida got up and looked about him. He saw an enormous hole in the flight deck just abaft the midships elevator. The elevator was twisted and wrecked, dropping down into the hangar deck. Deck plates were twisted upward from the impact of a bomb. Planes stood tail up, burning furiously. He heard the aviation officer shouting to him to get below and under cover, and he went down a ladder to the ready room. He found it full of wounded men. Another explosion shook the ship, and then more, and the whole ship trembled. Smoke from the fires on the hangar deck rushed through the passages, and forced them to leave the ready room. Commander Fuchida climbed back up onto the bridge. From there he could see that the *Kaga* and the *Soryu* were also hurt, giving off tall columns of smoke.

At Pearl Harbor Nimitz was seriously disturbed. The air battle must have reached its climax, and he knew absolutely nothing of what was happening out there by Midway. He called his communications officer and asked him where were the messages. But there were no messages. And the minutes kept ticking on. At 10:08 the radiomen at Pearl Harbor did hear the *Enterprise* air officer shout "Air attack," but that was all the information they had, and it did not indicate to whom the officer was speaking or anything else. Then they heard Lieutenant Commander Clarence McClusky say that he would attack as soon as he could find the enemy.

The *Hornet* dive-bombers, as noted, never did find the enemy. McClusky's *Enterprise* bombers did find the Japanese, and they attacked.

McClusky's squadron had no fighter cover; McClusky saw the enemy down below, maneuvering to escape the torpedo attack, which was just ending. McClusky struck with 37 planes of two squadrons; he sent one squadron against the *Kaga* and the other against the *Akagi*.

As Commander Fuchida had seen, the *Akagi* was hit three times, and one bomb was a near-miss and caused damage. One of the three hits was the elevator bomb, a 1,000-pounder that was the cause of the ultimate sinking of the ship. One of the bombs, the most spectacular, hit among the parked aircraft and started multiple fires. The reason the elevator bomb was so effective was that the Japanese had left their torpedoes and bombs on the hangar deck while rearming, and the American bombs started a whole series of explosions that literally blew the insides out of the carrier.

In less than half an hour it was apparent that there was no way of continuing the battle from this ship. Here is Admiral Kusaka's recollection as reported to the U.S. Strategic Bombing Survey Team after the war:

Admiral Nagumo thought the situation was under control and refused to come down from the bridge, but the captain of the ship [*Aoki*] advised him that the ship was out of control, that it should be abandoned and wanted him to abandon ship, but he refused. Admiral Nagumo was an extremely hot-tempered person and consequently he insisted on remaining on the bridge. I myself as chief of staff tried to convince him that as commander in chief it was his duty to abandon ship and transfer to some other ship where he could control the actions of the fleet, because it was no longer possible to communicate with other ships by wireless from the *Akagi*, and the signal flags and semaphore weren't sufficient to direct the battle.

Although Admiral Nagumo refused to come down, finally I had the others drag him by the hand and talk him into leaving the ship, but couldn't find a way down. Everything was so covered with smoke and flame. There was no way of getting down from the bridge except by a rope we hung from the bridge.

When I got down, the deck was on fire, and antiaircraft

and machine guns were firing automatically, having been set off by the fire aboard ship. Bodies were all over the place, and it wasn't possible to tell what would be shot up next.

Admiral Kusaka got off the ship, but he had his hands and feet burned in the process. Admiral Nagumo was unhurt. The staff was taken off by destroyer and transferred the flag to the light cruiser *Nagara*.

The battle of Midway continued.

CHAPTER TEN

Getting Back

In mid-morning, the first phase of the battle against the Japanese carriers was virtually over, and the American dive-bombers headed for home base. But at Pearl Harbor Admiral Nimitz and his staff were still completely in the dark. The radio intelligence did have a clue: the call sign of the command had shifted from the *Akagi* to a cruiser, and Commander Layton suggested that might mean the *Akagi* had been hurt, but he could not guarantee that to Nimitz. So at fleet headquarters, they waited impatiently.

By the time the American dive-bombers had finished their dives, the Japanese Zero fighters had begun to regroup, and when Commander McClusky pulled out of his dive, he found himself immediately pursued by two Zeros.

For 35 anxious miles, he kept the bomber skimming just above the surface of the sea. This created a difficult target for the Zeros, who shot at him with their 7.7-mm guns and then their 20-mm cannon. They put 58 holes in the airplane but it continued to fly. In the backseat, radio mechanic W. G. Chochalousek used his 30-caliber machine gun to shoot down one Zero that got too close. That event discouraged the other Zero, which then pulled away.

Lieutenant Commander John F. Thach's *Yorktown* fighter planes had escorted the carrier's torpedo planes to the target, but when they got there, the Wildcats found themselves fighting for their lives against the torpedoes of the Zeros, and they could do nothing to help the torpedo planes.

Up above the Japanese carriers, Lieutenant Commander

Thach had managed to re-form his half dozen fighters, and by close cooperation and aerobatics known as the "Thach weave" they were able to keep the Zeros at bay; as the dive-bombers came limping out of their attacks on the carriers, many of them hit by anti-aircraft fire, the fighters gave the bombers a bit of help on the way home.

When the last of the dive-bombers had cleared, Thach and four of his planes started back home with Lieutenant Commander Maxwell F. Leslie's dive-bombers.

The bombers were having their problems getting back to the carriers due to the miscalculations of Admiral Spruance's staff.

When the planes had flown off the carriers, they had word of point option. This was a line drawn on a chart with 15-minute intervals noted as to where the carrier was supposed to be at any given time. But this depended on the carrier maintaining at least an average course and speed, and the *Enterprise* and the *Hornet* had been forced to make many diversions in order to pick up and launch combat air patrol planes in the very light winds, so instead of making an average 24 knots on a course of 240 degrees, they averaged a little more than 12 knots. Thus when the pilots headed for the point option they could take, they found the carrier was not there, and since everyone was very carefully maintaining radio silence, the pilots were never told about the problem. McClusky's squadron reached their point option, but the carriers were 60 miles northeast. The planes were getting very low on gas, when McClusky spotted a carrier. It was the *Yorktown,* not his own, but any old port in a storm will do, and with two gallons of gasoline left in his tanks, McClusky landed aboard the *Yorktown*. But several other planes splashed into the sea.

Commander Leslie seems to have been the best navigator and the canniest thinker of the lot, for he figured the *Yorktown* would make about 12 knots; all his 17 dive-bombers made it back to their carrier, but they were held in a holding pattern above the *Yorktown* because Lieutenant Commander Thach's fighter planes were right behind them and the air officer of the *Yorktown* knew the fighters would be even lower on gas than the bombers.

Soon Thach landed, and found Admiral Fletcher on the bridge of the *Yorktown*. He made the first oral report of the battle, and told of leaving the scene with three of the four Japanese carriers burning.

Even Admiral Fletcher did not think to break radio silence to inform Admiral Nimitz of the progress of the battle. Not until Nimitz sent a message demanding some answers did Fletcher respond with the news that three carriers had been set afire by bombers. But then he made a serious mistake, saying that he had no indication of any other carriers in the Japanese fleet which had sighted the American force—when the fact was that Admiral Tamon Yamaguchi had indeed sighted the force and was sending an air strike to hit the Americans.

When the bombing of the *Akagi* had thrown the Japanese battle plan awry, the overall command of the striking force was automatically assumed by Rear Admiral Jiroaki Abe, the commander of Cruiser Division Eight in his flagship, the *Tone*. But command of air operations went to Rear Admiral Yamaguchi, who commanded the only carrier capable of air operations.

Yamaguchi was one of the comers of the Japanese navy, an honors graduate of the naval academy at Eta Jima and an airman. He was also much more aggressive than most of his superior officers, and during this fight he had already urged Admiral Nagumo to strike first, early that morning, but without success.

Now, however, Admiral Yamaguchi made a serious error. Aboard the *Hiryu* he had started operations with 63 aircraft, equally divided between fighters, dive-bombers, and torpedo bombers. Nearly all of these planes were still intact. Some of them were flying combat air patrol. But Admiral Yamaguchi did not send a full sortie; there were no torpedo bombers in the unit, just 18 dive-bombers and six fighters. It was a small strike for a large job.

Just a few minutes after Admiral Nagumo transferred his flag, Yamaguchi was ready to go.

CHAPTER ELEVEN

Nagumo Strikes Back

While Admiral Nagumo was taking his unscheduled ferry ride on the destroyer from the burning flagship *Akagi* to the light cruiser *Nagara*, he looked out across the eight miles of water where the Japanese ships were scattered about, and saw the *Soryu* and the *Kaga* burning fiercely. It was a chilling sight, but Nagumo decided that he would continue the battle from his one undamaged carrier, the *Hiryu*.

Aboard the *Nagara*, he tried to discover the condition of his carriers. He knew that the *Akagi* was very badly hit, and Admiral Kusaka kept telling him that she was doomed. But what about the *Kaga* and the *Soryu*?

A dozen dive-bombers from McClusky's two squadrons pinpointed the carrier *Kaga* and bored in on her. They began to score hits with 500-pound and 1,000-pound bombs. One bomb hit just forward of the ship's island bridge, and blew it to pieces, killing everyone, including the captain of the ship. Two other bombs set fire to the planes that crowded the deck, and a fourth bomb penetrated the hangar deck and started fires in the gasoline and bomb stowage rooms. Like the *Akagi*, the *Kaga* erupted in a mass of flame and secondary explosions caused by bombs and torpedoes going off and planes blowing up. That sure sign of a sense of destruction, the transfer of the emperor's portrait, was accomplished within the hour. Some officers and men jumped over the side and began to swim for it. Some stayed aboard to try to bring the fires under control.

Commander Amagai, the air officer of the *Kaga*, saw a periscope. The submarine (apparently the *Nautilus*) fired three torpedoes and one struck the *Kaga* a glancing blow, and the warhead, instead of exploding, fell off and sank, while the body of the torpedo floated, and several Japanese sailors clung to it for support.

Like the *Akagi,* the *Kaga*'s own guns were going off, firing ammunition at nothing in particular as the fires raged. Commander Amagai floated, clinging to flotsam, and was finally picked up by a destroyer.

Almost simultaneously with the *Enterprise* dive-bombers' attack on the *Akagi* and the *Kaga,* 17 dive-bombers from the *Yorktown* hit the *Soryu.* The *Hiryu,* the fourth Japanese carrier, was not bombed in this foray because in the maneuvering she had gotten out ahead of the others and was not seen.

Lieutenant Commander Leslie had led the *Yorktown* fliers on a more direct route to the carriers, so although the planes started later, they arrived at almost the same time.

The *Soryu* had just finished arming and fueling her share of the attack group that was going to strike the Americans. Her planes were lined up on the flight deck, and she was turning into the wind to launch, when the dive-bombers screamed down from 14,500 feet. The planes came down in three waves, approaching the bow and both sides. Three 1,000-pound bombs hit the carrier squarely. One went through the flight deck, ahead of the island, and exploded into the hangar deck, and pushed the forward elevator back against the ship's bridge. The second bomb struck amidships among the airplanes, blowing one Zero on the launching pad over the side, and starting fires in a dozen aircraft. The flight deck seemed to be one sheet of flame. Down below the bombs and torpedoes began to explode, and the ship's captain ordered the *Soryu* abandoned. He was last seen standing on his bridge. The American submarine *Nautilus* now got back into the fight, after that abortive attack on the *Kaga*. Just before 11:30 Lieutenant Commander W. H. Brockman, Jr., saw the burning carrier, and approached, although she was escorted by two destroyers. By this time, the fires aboard the ship had been brought under control and she was moving at about two knots. She had been abandoned, as ordered, but the executive officer had seen the fires diminishing and sent the damage control crew back aboard and they had brought the ship under control.

Command of the air strike from the *Hiryu* was entrusted to Lieutenant Michio Kobayashi. Here, again, the Japanese had chosen a highly qualified young officer, a veteran of the striking force's every action in this war. The planes took off and climbed to 12,000 feet, then headed toward the position where the *Tone* plane had sighted the enemy fleet. They had no problem, because they spotted Commander Leslie's bombers and followed them home, except that two of his fighter pilots decided to attack American planes and thus were lost from the strike force.

While that first attack group was going on, Admiral Yamaguchi ordered up a second strike. He had new information. A reconnaissance plane had landed on the *Hiryu* and the pilot told him there were not one, not two, but three American carriers! So Yamaguchi decided to go after another of them.

This time Admiral Yamaguchi was hard put to find the planes for the attack. The *Hiryu* and all the Japanese carriers had lost a number of planes in this busy day. What was available at the moment, using the planes in the hangar deck and those on deck, were 10 torpedo planes and six fighters. One of the torpedo planes was from the *Akagi*, which had landed aboard the *Hiryu* after the *Akagi* became inoperable. Two of the fighters were from the *Kaga*.

To lead this second strike Admiral Yamaguchi chose Lieutenant Joichi Tomonaga, who had participated in the raid on Midway—so, so long ago.

One of the fuel tanks of Tomonaga's plane had been damaged by antiaircraft fire on the Midway raid, and his plane handler pointed that out to him. Tomonaga shrugged and smiled. There was nothing to be done about that but fill up the other tank, and let that one go.

Some of the other fliers suggested that Tomonaga take one of their planes instead, but he refused. Everyone knew then that there was no way Tomonaga could return from this mission, and as they took off at 12:45 Admiral Yamaguchi watched sadly as did his staff on the bridge.

By that time Admiral Nagumo had moved his flag to the *Nagara* and had gotten his affairs in order and resumed tactical command of the operation.

Precisely at noon, Nagumo had a message from Lieutenant Kobayashi:

"We are bombing an enemy carrier."

Nagumo received another heartening message at that time, this one from Admiral Kondo, who announced that he was bringing his powerful force of two battleships, eight cruisers, and the light carrier *Zuiho,* plus a number of destroyers. And a few minutes later Admiral Yamamoto ordered the light carriers *Ryujo* and *Junyo* to leave the Aleutians area and hasten to help with the Midway operation.

At noon, Commander Leslie's dive-bombers were still orbiting the *Yorktown,* which had landed the fighters of the combat air patrol and Thach's fighters, and were hoping to land. But just then, after the *Yorktown* had launched 12 new fighters for combat air patrol, the word came that 30 or 40 planes were approaching the carrier about 40 miles out on the southwest. Leslie and his men were waved off, and the combat air patrol vectored out to meet the enemy, and the *Yorktown* speeded to 30 knots and prepared for action.

The combat air patrol was very effective; the pilots went after the Zeros and the dive-bombers and shot down most of them, but eight planes got through to make the attack. The combined antiaircraft fire of the cruisers and destroyers knocked down two more of the attacking planes, but six got through that obstacle and bombed. They got three hits on the *Yorktown*.

One bomb hit the flight deck and started fires there and on the hangar deck, but the damage control group opened the sprinkler system and extinguished the fires. Another bomb exploded in the smokestack, starting more fires and damaging the boilers and knocking out the fires in five of the six boilers. The ship immediately skidded to a slow speed. By 12:20 she was making only six knots. A third armor-piercing bomb exploded down on the fourth deck, starting fires near the gasoline

tanks and magazines. The magazines were flooded. The bomb
that went down the stack had wrecked communications on the
bridge, so Admiral Fletcher had to lift his flag to the cruiser
Astoria. He wanted the cruiser *Portland* to take the *Yorktown*
in tow, but it was not necessary. By 1:30 that afternoon four
of the six boilers were working again, and she began making
20 knots.

The flight operations were resumed and she began to fuel
fighters. Then came another ominous warning. The second
Hiryu strike was on its way and was just 40 miles out.

From the horizon, Admiral Spruance had seen the smoke
from the fires aboard the *Yorktown* and had detached two cruisers and two destroyers to join Fletcher and provide additional
antiaircraft fire.

The fueling had not been fast enough. The *Yorktown* managed to get eight fighters into the air, but most of them had
only enough gasoline to stay up a few minutes. So at the
moment there were 12 fighters up, with an incoming strike
nine miles out at 2:30 in the afternoon.

The Japanese torpedo attack was masterful. First of all, the
Japanese Nakajima 97 torpedo bomber was far superior in
speed and performance to the American TBF Avenger. Second,
the Japanese pilots were superb; they had trained at least five
years for this moment and they came in fearlessly from four
directions, coming up to perhaps 500 yards from the carrier
before releasing their torpedoes. The *Yorktown* maneuvered
and managed to avoid two of the torpedoes, but two others hit
on the port side, breaking up the fuel tanks, jamming the
rudder, and breaking the power circuits. She immediately took
a list of 16 degrees, which increased very rapidly to 26 degrees.

The captain of the *Yorktown* feared that the ship was about
to capsize, and since the ship had no power, they could do
nothing to counterflood. Just before 3:00 P.M., he ordered the
ship abandoned. Four destroyers came up to take off the crew.
Some men went into the sea, but all were rescued.

Lieutenant Kobayashi, after the first strike, had radioed
triumphantly back to the Japanese fleet that they had left the
Yorktown a blazing wreck, and it was true at the time. Ko-

bayashi did not stay around long enough to see the carrier put back into shape, and his plane was one of those lost in the action. Only five Japanese planes made it back, and their accounts were fragmentary.

The *Yorktown* had survived the first attack, but after this second attack it was a different story. Yamaguchi had in the interim learned of the existence of the two more carriers in the American contingent, and that second strike had been aimed at the second carrier; a reconnaissance plane had landed aboard the *Hiryu* and Admiral Yamaguchi learned to his surprise that there was not one, or two, carriers, but three in the American force, and so he sent the second strike.

Just before 2:30 the fliers radioed back to the *Hiryu* that they were attacking a *Yorktown*-class carrier, but they did not know that it actually was the *Yorktown* again, for they thought she had been sunk.

At 4:40 in the afternoon, the surviving planes returned to the *Hiryu* and Admiral Yamaguchi had the story of the attack. Only five bombers and three fighters returned, and, as expected, Tomonaga was not one of them. A fellow pilot described his end:

> His plane with its distinguishing yellow tail was clearly discernible as he broke through the heaviest antiaircraft fire I have ever witnessed. He launched his torpedo, and then in the next instant his plane was disintegrated. His assault on the carrier, in the face of that devastating gunfire, was tantamount to a suicide crash.

So the Japanese believed they had hit and sunk two American carriers, when in fact they had simply hit one carrier twice.

CHAPTER TWELVE

The Last Air Attack

Late in the morning, Admiral Fletcher had sent out a search force of 10 dive-bombers. They were heading back for their carrier at 2:45 when one pilot spotted the *Hiryu,* two battleships, three cruisers, and four destroyers steaming north about a hundred miles from the *Yorktown.* They reported back, and 45 minutes later, Admiral Spruance ordered an attack by planes from the *Enterprise.* Twenty-four dive-bombers were sent off, without fighter escort because all the fighters were needed for the combat air patrol that afternoon.

When the ragged remnants of the *Hiryu*'s second strike straggled home to the carrier at 4:30 that afternoon, Yamaguchi could count only six fighters, five dive-bombers, and four torpedo bombers left of his carrier's air force after three missions and a day of combat air patrols. Since morning, the *Hiryu* had been attacked by 79 planes, and had evaded 26 torpedoes and 70 bombs. The ship's crew and the aircrews were all but exhausted, but Admiral Yamaguchi planned another attack with his remaining aircraft, for a twilight approach to the enemy. The men must have a meal, however, and just before 5:00 P.M. sweet rice balls were served out to the crew at their action stations. Above, the combat air patrol continued, and below on the hangar deck, the handlers made preparations for the last strike of the day.

At a few minutes past 5 P.M. Admiral Yamaguchi prepared to send a special fast reconnaissance plane of a new type, which had been part of the *Kaga* contingent, out to locate what the admiral believed to be the last remaining American carrier.

But as the plane was preparing to take off, the lookouts piped up:

"Enemy dive-bombers directly overhead."

The Americans had cleverly come in from the southwest with the sun directly behind them, and since the Japanese carriers had no radar, they had not been detected.

The captain immediately began furious evasive action, and the first turn, with full right rudder, enabled the ship to avoid three bombs, which fell nearby. But then the other planes from the *Enterprise* were diving on the *Hiryu* and they made four direct hits, all of them near the bridge. The forward elevator was blasted upward so that it obstructed the view of the control room. Fires spread among the planes on the deck and cut off the engine room from the rest of the ship. The engine room crew kept working and trying to fight the fires until one by one they were overcome by smoke and flame.

The carrier planes also attacked the cruisers and battleships of the fleet, but scored no hits, nor did land-based aircraft which came a little later score any.

The planes in this attack on the *Hiryu* were partly from the *Enterprise*, but some of them were *Yorktown* planes that had landed on the *Enterprise* after their own carrier was damaged. Three bombers were lost in the air strike.

So by 5:15 on the afternoon of June 4, the battle of Midway was won; the Japanese had lost four carriers and at that point the Americans had lost none.

That afternoon the *Akagi* continued to burn and at 5:15 as the *Hiryu* was under attack, the captain finally ordered the *Akagi* abandoned, but she did not sink.

The *Hiryu* burned and burned, and at 9:00 P.M. she slowed and finally stopped. The list was then 15 degrees. Other ships stood by and helped fight the fires but at 2:30 on the morning of June 5, Admiral Yamaguchi summoned the hands and gave a little speech.

As commanding officer of this carrier division, I am fully and solely responsible for the loss of *Hiryu* and *Soryu*. I shall remain on board to the end. I command all of you to leave the ship and continue your loyal service to the emperor.

Captain Kaku also elected to go down with the ship and so all the others departed and the two officers remained on the bridge as the ship drifted slowly in the light sea. The destroyers *Kazugumo* and *Yugumo* then torpedoed the *Hiryu*, and slowly she went down just as dawn was breaking.

Meanwhile, Admiral Yamamoto in the flagship *Yamato* was as much in the dark about the progress of the battle as was Admiral Nimitz.

That night of June 4 there might have been a night surface battle between opposing fleets if the situation had developed a little differently than it did.

On the morning of June 4 the flagship and the main body of the Japanese fleet were heading east at a point 800 miles northwest of Midway. Sunrise came just before 5 A.M., but the fleet did not see it; the whole area was shrouded in thick fog. But just after 5:30 the sun peeped through and Yamamoto ordered the fleet to refuel. Just before six came the word that the *Tone*'s observation plane had sighted American carrier planes. Then came the report from Lieutenant Tomonaga that he had made his strike on Midway and another was needed. Yamamoto and his staff then waited confidently for word that the second strike had been made and the air power of Midway was destroyed.

The admiral had been sick and cranky with a stomach ailment the day before but he was recovered and in good spirits on June 4, supremely confident that his plan would carry and Midway would be occupied and the American fleet lured out and destroyed.

But then the *Tone* plane that morning announced the sighting of 10 ships, and a little later came the inclusion in the report of a carrier.

Ships . . . carrier?

Where had those ships come from? There weren't supposed to be any ships anywhere near Midway.

For a few minutes this news caused concern in the staff. Somebody had certainly made a big mistake, not to find these ships long before this time.

But these musings were cut short when the *Tone* plane reported another pair of enemy cruisers 250 miles northeast of Midway. Admiral Ugaki radiated confidence and spoke glowingly of Admiral Nagumo and his ability to handle the situation. Privately Admiral Yamamoto disagreed—he had very little use for Nagumo—but he said nothing.

Next that morning came the news that 10 enemy planes were heading for the Nagumo force. But air officer Sasaki said that the combat air patrol should have no difficulty in dealing with them. The confidence of the Combined Fleet staff was enormous, another sign of the "Victory disease" that afflicted most of Japan and had since Pearl Harbor Day.

Captain Kuroshima, the senior staff officer, asked Admiral Ugaki, the chief of staff, if Admiral Nagumo's plan for the second attack wave would not disrupt the plan to save that second wave for a strike against ships. The air officer, Commander Sasaki, said yes, but Commander Miwa, the operations officer, pointed out that Nagumo had already launched the second strike at Midway. So the flagship staff was confused and asked if there was any indication that the second strike had been sent to Midway. It had not, said the radio room. So everyone heaved a sigh of relief and waited for word that the American carrier or carriers had been destroyed.

Then came the blow. Commander Yushiro Wada, the staff communications officer, did not have the heart to speak when he came up to Admiral Yamamoto with the message. He simply handed it over. It was from Admiral Abe in the cruiser *Tone*, who had taken temporary command while Admiral Nagumo was shifting from the burning *Akagi* to the cruiser *Nagara*:

Fires raging aboard *Kaga*, *Soryu*, and *Akagi* resulting from enemy attacks by carrier and land-based planes. We plan to have *Hiryu* engage enemy carriers. We are temporarily withdrawn to the north to assemble our forces.

The jubilation that had settled on the bridge was gone, replaced by the blackest despair. No one said anything. No one offered any ideas. But Admiral Yamamoto pulled himself together.

There was only one solution, he said, and that was to concentrate the full force of the Combined Fleet at this point and overwhelm the American fleet. They still had the light carrier *Zuiho,* and the light carriers *Ryujo* and *Junyo* with the Aleutians force, and three seaplane carriers. The admiral knew he could outclass the enemy in battleships and cruisers.

And so Admiral Yamamoto decided to rush to the scene with his main body and personally direct the battle to a victory for Japan.

It was an hour before the main fleet could get organized and complete the fueling. And then the course was set at 120 degrees and the ships worked up to 20 knots.

As he went, Yamamoto ordered his forces to close around him, the Aleutians invasion force to stand by and the Aleutians covering force to join at Midway with its now-precious light carriers. The admiral was still confident of victory as he ordered the Midway invasion force to stand by and wait for developments.

Admiral Yamamoto needed some information. He wanted to know the American land-based air strength at Midway following that first strike.

Admiral Ugaki sent a message to Admiral Nagumo asking for details of the success of the Midway attack and how much strength the Americans had left there. He received no reply to this inquiry and Yamamoto then concluded that the attack could not have been very successful. He was concerned lest the Americans send in more planes and make Midway even harder to capture. Of course he did not know that except for the B-17 bombers based there and the PBYs, the Midway air force was down to less than a half dozen planes.

Captain Kuroshima suggested that they send a strong surface force to Midway to bombard the island during the night, thus destroying any new aircraft that might have arrived, and also battering the shore facilities. Admiral Yamamoto accepted that suggestion as logical and necessary and issued orders. In the planning of the Midway operation, the possibility of disaster had not been ignored, and one of the alternative methods of achieving overall victory was outlined in what the Japanese referred to as Attack Method C, which would utilize all the elements of the Aleutians invasion force and the main body of the fleet, as well as the Midway invasion force and the Nagumo striking force. Yamamoto now issued that order, and another order to Admiral Kondo to send battleships and cruisers to bombard Midway. Until this was done the landing operations at Midway would be postponed.

The fact was that as of the afternoon of June 4, if Admiral Yamamoto could assemble his forces, and could bombard Midway, knocking out the PBYs, B-26 bombers, B-17s, the half dozen Buffalo fighters, five FSFs, and 14 dive-bombers left there, Yamamoto might still win the air battle. For as of that moment, the *Yorktown* was not operational, and the *Enterprise* and the *Hornet* between them (with some planes having landed at Midway) could mount only 135 aircraft. The Japanese, while using their light carriers and seaplane carriers—the *Zuiho, Hosho, Ryujo,* and *Junyo,* and the seaplane carriers *Chitose, Kamikawa,* and *Kimikawa Maru*—could put up 155 planes. The problem was to assemble and utilize this force.

But already as Yamamoto issued his orders to do battle, he had word that Admiral Nagumo was planning to retire to the north, and abandon the invasion. An hour after Yamamoto sent out his orders he heard more from Nagumo, demanding that Rear Admiral Kakuta bring the light carriers *Ryujo* and *Junyo* down to bolster the Nagumo force.

But Admiral Kakuta was not encouraging in his reply to that demand. From his position, 120 miles southwest of Dutch Harbor, Alaska, he could not arrive off Midway before the afternoon of June 8. Had the planners wanted to allow for possible disaster, they should have arranged for Kakuta to strike earlier or later and have him ready to join the Midway battle if necessary. But in the euphoria of "Victory" the possibility of defeat had been glossed over. Indeed, in the tabletop maneuvers conducted twice before the Midway invasion, Admiral

Ugaki, the chief of staff, had intervened, cheated in effect, to show victory where defeat had been indicated. Without the planes of the *Ryujo* and the *Junyo,* the Japanese could mount only 65 aircraft including the float planes, and the float planes of the cruisers and battleships, which could be used for bombing although they were hardly ideal for the purpose.

On the heels of the discouraging information about Admiral Kakuta's position came good news from Admiral Yamaguchi, who reported that his planes had damaged two of the three American carriers he knew to exist.

At 5:30 a search plane from the cruiser *Chikuma* placed the American force about a hundred miles east of Nagumo with his battleships and cruisers, which would make it possible for Nagumo and Kondo to engage in night action.

But a few minutes later, the news that *Hiryu* had been put out of action sent despair through the Combined Fleet staff. Admiral Yamamoto, however, did not despair, but called for Nagumo to strike the enemy, while the main body moved up to do the same. He wanted a night fight. Nagumo then intervened with a report that he must have known was a lie: "The enemy strength is five carriers, six heavy cruisers, and 15 destroyers. They are steaming westward. We are retiring to the northwest, escorting *Hiryu*. Speed 18 knots."

The fact was that Nagumo was retiring, but he was not escorting the *Hiryu*. She had been left behind with the destroyers *Kazugumo* and *Yugumo*.

When Admiral Ugaki read the Nagumo message he recognized it immediately for what it was. "The Nagumo force has not enough stomach for a night engagement," he said.

Seeing that, Admiral Yamamoto removed Nagumo from command, and put Admiral Kondo in charge. This, to all effects, ended Admiral Nagumo's naval career. He would go on to command one or two carriers at Guadalcanal, but there would perform so miserably that he would end up his days on Saipan and be lost in the last battle for that island.

Admiral Kondo then headed toward the Americans, and ordered Admiral Nagumo to come along and fight, but when Admiral Yamamoto checked the positions, he could see that there was no way Kondo could reach the Americans before dawn. So the last hope of victory died out.

What to do now?

Aboard the *Yamato* the Combined Fleet staff pondered the problem. Air officer Sasaki suggested that they employ the planes of the light carriers and the seaplane carriers, to replace those of the lost fleet carriers, and hold the American carriers at bay until the battleships could destroy them. The gunnery officer advocated an even longer and stronger bombardment, to neutralize Midway and make the landings possible. Another staff officer said to ignore the American carriers and proceed with the landings. The combined antiaircraft fire of the battleships and cruisers, he said, would drive off any air attacks.

(The fallacy of this argument was shown decisively at Leyte Gulf's battle of Samar, when planes of the Third Fleet virtually wiped out the Japanese fleet.)

The staff officers drew up a plan and presented it to Admiral Ugaki. He took one look and recognized that it was foolhardy.

The stupidity of engaging such shore installations with a surface force ought to be clear to you. The airfield at Midway is still usable, a large number of American planes are based there, and some of the enemy carriers are still intact. Our battleships, for all their firepower, would be destroyed by enemy air and submarine attacks before we could even get close enough for our big guns.

If circumstances permit, we will be able to launch another offensive after the Second Carrier Striking Force has joined. But even if that proves impossible, and we must accept defeat in this operation, we will not have lost the war. There will still be eight carriers in the fleet, counting those which are to be completed soon. So we should not lose heart. In battle as in chess it is the fool who lets himself be led into a reckless move through desperation.

The young members of the staff did not like what they heard. ''But how can we apologize to His Majesty for this defeat?'' they asked.

Admiral Yamamoto then spoke up:

"Leave that to me," he ordered. "I am the only one who must apologize to His Majesty."

So just after midnight ushered in the fifth of June, Admiral Yamamoto ordered Admiral Kondo and Admiral Nagumo to suspend operations and join up with the main body of the fleet. The transports would also join up. The Midway operation was over.

CHAPTER THIRTEEN

The Sinking of the Yorktown

The Americans knew from their radio interceptions the general plan of the Midway attack, but they had no idea that Admiral Yamamoto would bring the entire Combined Fleet to Midway. Thus on the night of June 4–5, when the admiral broke radio silence and sent a string of messages to the fleet, calling them home, the American radio interceptors for the first time understood that Yamamoto and the *Yamato* were actually near Midway, with a force of battleships and cruisers far superior to the American. This settled a dispute that had been simmering all day and evening: whether or not Admiral Spruance, having sunk the four carriers, should give chase that night to the other ships of the fleet and hope to catch more of them with American planes, and possibly with surface and submarine attack.

Spruance had refused to do this. The pilot had reported seeing Zeros flying around the burning *Hiryu* in late afternoon, and Spruance was not even sure they did not come from the carrier. They must have been the *Hiryu*'s own planes from the combat air patrol, which had nowhere to land, but there was no way Admiral Spruance could know that. So he rejected the idea of a night engagement, and withdrew the two carriers *Hornet* and *Enterprise* to the east. Had he pursued, he would have run smack into the heavy concentration of cruisers and battleships, and he did not have a single battleship. So in this particular case, with the radio intelligence intercepts not giving the whole story, the Americans were very lucky to have a conservative admiral in charge of operations. If Spruance had run into the Japanese battleships, his carriers might have been sunk and then there would be nothing to prevent the Japanese from carrying out the original plan.

The next day, when Nimitz learned that Yamamoto and the whole fleet were out there, he was surprised, and his faith in the radio intelligence was turned back a couple of notches. But because of Spruance's caution, it worked out well for the Americans.

So the Japanese had decided to head home. In response to the order from Admiral Yamamoto, Admiral Kurita's four cruisers and two destroyers turned back from their earlier assigned mission to bombard Midway; at about 2:15 on the morning of June 5, they were sighted about a hundred miles west of the atoll by the American submarine *Tambor*. The cruisers also sighted the submarine and Admiral Kurita ordered an emergency turn of the ship column, but the cruiser *Mogami* did not get the word, and in turning rammed into the cruiser *Mikuma*. Both ships were badly damaged. The *Mikuma* caught fire. Her bow was smashed in and she was unable to make more than 12 knots thereafter. She also had an oil leak and moved along the sea leaving a telltale wake for submarines or aircraft. Admiral Kurita left them behind with the two destroyers for screen and moved ahead to obey his orders and join up with Yamamoto.

Earlier in the day, when he thought about attacking Midway again, Admiral Yamamoto had ordered the submarine *I-168* to shell the island installations until Admiral Kurita could come up with his cruiser force. The orders had been countermanded, but the *I-168* came anyhow and began shelling, and failed to hit anything. All her shells dropped in the lagoon. So she went away.

On the morning of June 5, as the sun came up, all the 31 PBYs that could fly were sent aloft to start searching for the Japanese. One pilot of a flying boat sighted the *Mikuma* oil slick and the two cruisers and their destroyer escorts, and notified Midway. Captain Simard then sent the B-17s to attack but they could not find the ships. So Simard then sent out the marine bombing squadron. They could put together only six SBDs, and only six SBU bombers were ready to fly. They found the oil slick and trailed it until they came to the cruisers. They attacked by dive-bombing and glide bombing. But the Japanese ships put up a hail of antiaircraft fire, and only one plane scored, in a sacrificial way. Captain Richard T. Fleming crashed into the after turret of the *Mikuma*, but all the other bombers missed or near-missed.

When the *Tambor*'s report about sighting the Kurita force was received aboard the *Enterprise*, Admiral Spruance decided to head back for Midway to give air support to the island the next day in case the Japanese attacked.

At 6:00 A.M. Spruance began to receive reports of several ship dispositions, including two damaged cruisers.

The reports were contradictory and confusing, and gave the impression that there were still two carriers out there somewhere.

At three o'clock in the afternoon Spruance sent out 58 planes to try to find carriers up north. There were no carriers so they did not find them; they did, however, run across a destroyer which they attacked, but lost one plane for their trouble and did not hit the destroyer.

So June 5 ended with no decisive actions.

The next day, the planes went after the crippled cruisers *Mogami* and *Mikuma*. Shortly after dawn, reconnaissance planes found the two cripples. Three air strikes were launched from two working American carriers, a total of 112 planes.

On the first attack, the *Mogami* was hit twice by bombs, and twice again in the second, and again in the third, and she was badly damaged. One engine room was virtually burned out and one turret was destroyed, but she continued to steam on toward Truk.

The *Mikuma* was so badly damaged in the first two attacks that the captain ordered her abandoned. The destroyer *Arashiuo* picked men out of the water, but when the third air attack came that afternoon, many of those survivors were killed on the deck of the destroyer by a bomb. Another bomb hit the *Mikuma* and started her torpedoes exploding. She was abandoned by the screen destroyers then, and sank that night.

What Admiral Yamamoto feared had also come about: many army B-17 bombers had been flown in from Hawaii. However, because of the lack of training of the pilots in work at sea, they proved to be more a nuisance than a help, and bombed the American submarine *Grayling* and forced her to crash-dive to survive.

At the end of the day on June 6, Admiral Spruance surveyed his situation. His pilots had been flying for three days and were exhausted. His four destroyers were very low on fuel.

The task force was 400 miles west of Midway and heading into enemy territory where it would not be too long before shore-based aircraft could challenge them. So he turned back east, and brought the battle of Midway to an end.

Admiral Yamamoto continued to hope that Spruance would be lured to within striking distance of his land-based aircraft and would somehow offer the opportunity for a surface engagement, which most certainly would be won by the superior firepower of the Japanese battleships. But he could not tempt Spruance, so he began to fuel and then started the long trip home to Japan.

The carrier *Yorktown*, abandoned after the second Japanese attack, continued to float and some who understood survival and salvage wondered why she had ever been abandoned. Admiral Fletcher in the cruiser *Astoria* started east, leaving the destroyer *Hughes* to watch over the *Yorktown* and to sink her with torpedoes if it seemed possible she might be captured by the enemy. The commander of the *Hughes* notified Admiral Nimitz that in his opinion the *Yorktown* could be saved. At one point Admiral Fletcher had talked about having her towed by the cruiser *Portland*, but it was not done. Instead, from Pearl Harbor, Admiral Nimitz sent the fleet tug *Navajo*, the minesweeper *Vireo*, and the destroyer *Gwin*. The *Vireo* arrived first and put a line on the carrier, but could scarcely make headway with the tow. The *Gwin* arrived and put a salvage party aboard the carrier. Anchors and other heavy weights were jettisoned to lighten the load.

Finally on this second day Admiral Fletcher decided to send a proper salvage party aboard the carrier, and sent about 200 men in the destroyer *Hammann*.

Just before dawn the *Hammann* tied up on the starboard side of the carrier and transferred the salvage party and provided power and pumps for the work of righting the carrier from its list. One fire was still burning and this was put out. By mid-afternoon on June 6, progress was being made and those aboard felt sure the carrier could be saved. Several destroyers circled the carrier about a mile out.

The Americans did not know it but the *Yorktown* was being stalked. On June 5, a cruiser's seaplane had spotted the carrier drifting, and Admiral Yamamoto had ordered the submarine *I-168* to find the carrier and sink her. The plane's pilot had given the wrong coordinates, but after a search for 24 hours, the skipper of *I-168* saw the several destroyers and the carrier, and began to make an approach early on the afternoon of June 6. He managed to get through the destroyer screen without being observed or heard. At 1:30 in the afternoon he fired four torpedoes. One exploded on the side of the *Hammann*, and broke her in two; she sank in minutes with great loss of lives. Two torpedoes went under the keel of the destroyer and exploded against the starboard side of the carrier.

The *Vireo* cut the towline, and the salvage party was moved to the destroyer *Benham*. Captain Buckmaster of the *Yorktown*, who was directing the salvage, intended to start again at dawn, but during the night the ship's list grew much worse and at dawn it was evident that there was no saving her. Soon she rolled over and sank.

That was the end of the battle, but not the end of Admiral Spruance's carrier operations.

Although the *Yorktown* was gone, Admiral Nimitz still had three carriers in the Pacific: the *Saratoga* had been repaired from its torpedo damage, and Rear Admiral Aubrey W. Fitch had brought her to Pearl Harbor. There she was loaded with replacement planes for the *Enterprise* and the *Hornet* and sent to meet Spruance and turn over the planes. Spruance then set sail with 34 replacement planes and moved toward the Aleutians, but then Nimitz had a change of mind and ordered the task force back to Pearl Harbor.

CHAPTER FOURTEEN

The Meaning of Midway

The American victory at the battle of Midway made a major change in the Pacific war. Or, one should say, major changes. In the first place, it raised a sagging American morale which was enormously important. If matters had continued to go as they had been in the first six months of the war, perhaps President Roosevelt would have felt impelled to change his position to fight Germany first, and would thus have had American resources concentrated in the Pacific as many Americans wanted to do, largely on the principle that European affairs had little to do with the United States.

The defeat of the Japanese was immediately recognized by all those who knew the facts as a real defeat, and it deflated the enormous ego that the Japanese military machine had built up, although it did not stop the flood of propaganda. Later, as the times changed, the Japanese propaganda became more outrageous, less truthful, and less useful in the long run for Japan's own ambitions.

Physically, the defeat of the Japanese fleet meant that the Americans would not have to face those four fleet carriers which had been sunk. That was an enormous difference, because while Admiral Yamamoto put the best face on it, by talking about the eight Japanese carriers actually in existence and being built, in reality they were reduced to four major carriers. Moreover, the *Shinano,* the supercarrier that had been first designed as a super-battleship, would never enter the war, but would be sunk ignominiously by an American submarine in Japanese waters during its trials. So Midway was Japan's last chance to overwhelm the Americans with supremacy of carriers.

After that date, the fleet was much more cautious in its commitment of its vanishing resources; while the Americans were just gearing up to produce a dozen carriers, the Japanese had no such resources, and would have to fight the war basically with the weapons that were available at the outset. That was why Admiral Yamamoto told his compatriots that he needed a quick victory, for he knew that a war of attrition would end in a Japanese defeat.

At Midway, he must have seen that defeat staring him in the face, and thereafter, although he went valiantly to the South Pacific when the time came and spent the rest of his life there, as he knew he would, he had little hope of ultimate victory.

The superiority of Japan's navy really disappeared on June 4, 1942, when the *Hiryu*, the *Soryu,* the *Kaga*, and the flagship *Akagi* all went down before the assault of American aircraft and submarines. In the Guadalcanal campaign that followed, the Japanese had superiority in the beginning because of their major fleet air base at Rabaul and the satellite airfields in the Solomons. They also had surface ship superiority for a time, but the Americans were furiously building carriers, battleships, and cruisers, and by the autumn of 1943 were able to put 11 major carriers and three escort carriers behind the Gilbert Island landings. Thereafter, the naval issue was really no longer in doubt. The Americans continued to build until the end of the war; they might have lost four carriers in a single battle without it affecting the outcome, so great was their carrier superiority.

The key to the American victory in the battle of Midway was the American intelligence breaking of the Japanese naval code—but it was no more than a key. The Japanese arrived with air superiority in carriers. The American shore-based air-force at Midway proved to be singularly ineffective, and the American torpedo bombers, most of them lost in the battle, did not score any hits at all. The Japanese had superior fighter planes, superior torpedo bombers, and dive-bombers that equaled the American in strength. Why then, even given the advantage of the code break, did the Americans win?

The answer lies in bad Japanese planning for the whole operation. The Combined Fleet was the most powerful in the world just then. Had Admiral Yamamoto put all his power against Midway, with three more light carriers, the result might have been very different.

But the real error was Admiral Nagumo's in not taking care of assuming that his enemies might be anywhere at all, including right on top of him. If the Japanese had been aware of the presence of the American carriers two hours earlier, as they might have been had their search pattern been proper, they would not have been surprised between air strikes, and they might have gotten the first blow in themselves. Then the superiority of the weapons would have counted.

And, even allowing for the loss of the carriers, had the whole force been operating together, including the force diverted to the Aleutians, then a night attack would have been possible and it was well-known that the Japanese were superior to the Americans in night fighting.

In their study of Midway, Mitsuo Fuchida and Masatake Okumiya suggest that if Admiral Yamamoto had directed the operation himself, and kept the main body with the carriers, they might not have been lost—at least not all of them. The enormous antiaircraft firepower of the battleships themselves might have diverted some of the bombers from the carrier targets.

Admiral Nagumo did not remember that the basic reason for Midway was not the capture of the Pacific island to be used as an advance air base, but to draw out and destroy the American fleet.

But the primary fault lay further back, with the plan itself, and the employment of the same group of carriers for two purposes.

If the main purpose of Midway was to destroy the American fleet, as Admiral Yamamoto said, then the fleet should have been completely mobile and dedicated to that purpose. Had the *Zuikaku* and the *Shokaku* been along, or had the Combined Fleet utilized three or four light carriers in their absence, then the big carriers could have been freed from the task of "softening up" Midway, and left to their real task.

Some officers, including Admiral Kondo, had suggested that the whole operation be postponed, as the Coral Sea battle had made it impossible to employ the *Zuikaku* and the *Shokaku*. The reasons given by the Combined Fleet staff against change were the meteorological conditions and the tides at Midway in this particular period. But Admiral Yamamoto's secret reason was more compelling. He was driven by the need for a quick victory over the Americans, knowing that every day of delay gave the enemy greater chance to recover. Understanding the enemy's enormous productive resources, Yamamoto knew that if they had delayed six months, the Americans would have more carriers for him to face on the seas.

The Midway plan called for the Japanese submarines to go to French Frigate Shoals, as they had done once before, and send aloft a submarine-carried aircraft to scout Pearl Harbor. But Nimitz learned of the plan through radio intercepts, and sent American ships there first, which made it impossible for the Japanese to carry out that plan. However, once the plan had miscarried, it made all the more important the search by the carrier task force itself, and this was not recognized or carried out.

The Japanese critics pointed out that Admiral Nagumo committed three serious blunders. First was his failure to be sure that the searches on the morning of the strike were thorough. Commander Fuchida was aghast to learn that the two-phase search that was carrier doctrine had not been carried out. But the lesser commanders, the ship captains, should have made sure that their planes got off on time, and if they had not, then Nagumo should have been informed of the details so he could have adjusted his plans. Nor were the pilots of the planes very careful in the searches. The pilot of the *Chikuma* plane flew right over the enemy fleet and did not see it.

Admiral Nagumo's second big error was to split up his forces. He should have used two of his big carriers to mount the Midway strike, thus leaving all the planes of two other carriers free for the strike against the enemy fleet when and if it appeared. By using planes from all carriers he got his strike off earlier, but that was not important; what was important was that the business of utilizing all four carriers all at the same time made the fleet much more vulnerable. Since all four carriers were involved in sending off planes for the Midway strike, then all four carriers had to shut down dispatch of planes at the same time to recover planes from the strike. This greatly reduced their capability of striking the enemy.

Nagumo's third and fatal error was to fail to launch a strike against the enemy at the moment that he learned there was a carrier involved. As of that point he would still have enjoyed the "surprise gauge," the equivalent in carrier warfare to the "weather gauge" of sailing ships, where the ship that had the favorable wind was given a great advantage. The reason given for waiting was to secure fighter protection. But the Americans launched and sent forth bombers without protection several times during the fight. The Americans were right, the first thing to do was be first. Admiral Yamaguchi recognized that fact and urged Admiral Nagumo to strike the moment he heard the word. But Nagumo played the orthodox admiral; there should be fighters to accompany the bombers.

In fact, there was nothing orthodox about carrier warfare, and the outcome of Midway—brought about by the sacrifice of the American torpedo bombers setting up the success of the dive-bombers—is proof of that point. Anything can happen in warfare, but to paraphrase Lord Nelson, the carrier task force commander who got his planes in to attack his enemy first had to be doing something right.

These errors stemmed partly from Nagumo's own character. He was a conservative man, a battleship man who did not really understand the use of carriers or the vital factors of their employment. He had already shown that at Pearl Harbor and Trincomalee; both had presented opportunities to do much more damage.

The second factor, however, and equally important, was the "victory disease" that afflicted the carrier task force. They had been told so often by their naval comrades and the Japanese media that they were great that they had come to believe it.

Yamamoto did *not* believe; he did not trust Nagumo, particularly after Pearl Harbor, but under the Japanese naval system, Yamamoto, though chief of the Combined Fleet, did not have power over the selection of subordinate commanders. That power remained in the hands of Tokyo.

The other great problem of the Midway defeat was what to do after the four carriers were lost. In fact, not much could be done because the forces were so badly scattered. Someone should have played devil's advocate a long time before, and totted up all the possible disasters that could have happened to the fleet. A few officers tried, but there the Japanese staff system came into play. Admiral Yamamoto, once he had made his plan and had persuaded the higher authorities in Tokyo to accept it, turned the operation of the plan over to his chief of staff, Admiral Ugaki, and the Combined Fleet staff. They had a vested interest in its success, and in the war games that preceded the operations; they loaded the dice so that the results came out as they wanted them to, not as they might possibly have occurred if chance had been left to decide, as was planned.

And once the carriers were gone, could Admiral Yamamoto have fought on with the two Aleutians carriers, plus the two light carriers left to him? As it turned out he could have, because the Americans milled around for a while and did not immediately rush to Pearl Harbor or anywhere else. The carrier *Saratoga* brought planes to refurbish the two Midway carriers, the *Enterprise* and the *Hornet*, but they did not arrive to deliver the planes until late on June 7. Admiral Kakuta could have arrived before then and helped carry out an attack.

The fact seems to be that Admiral Yamamoto was so stricken by the failure of his plan and his inability to come to grips with the American fleet on his own terms that his iron resolution wavered, and in the vacillation the chance was lost. A little later, reconsidering, he tried to lure the American fleet toward Wake, planning to use the carriers *Zuiho* and *Hosho* and land-based air for this purpose.

Japanese critics have complained that the Japanese naval concept of command was also partly responsible for the defeat at Midway. Admiral Yamamoto, they aver, should have kept his headquarters in Tokyo instead of aboard the battleship *Yamato*. The argument for the *Yamato* was that thus the commander in chief served as an inspiration for the fleet. The argument against it is that communications were difficult and when the *Yamato* was at sea on the operation, the admiral was constrained by radio silence not to give any information to Admiral Nagumo, and Nagumo did not know that the Americans were out long before the Japanese got to Midway. These critics point to the fact that Admiral Nimitz's headquarters were ashore during the entire war, first at Pearl Harbor and then at Guam.

But the fact is that in the Midway operation Nimitz, like Yamamoto, was kept in the dark about what was actually going on, although, like Yamamoto, Nimitz was really in command of the operation. Neither the American nor the Japanese admiral wanted to interfere with the people on the scene, on the theory that they knew better than anyone else what was going on.

In the matter of the inept employment of the Japanese carriers at Midway, one solution could have been to use the Japanese battleships for the purpose of "softening up" Midway with an extended bombardment before the landing operations. That would have freed the carriers for the fleet action and might have made all the difference. But the Japanese at that point considered capital ships to be best used in facing other capital ships, not realizing that with the coming of the carrier age that was not very likely to happen often. So the opportunity was lost.

The Imperial Navy also had a personnel policy regarding air matters that caused an enormous amount of difficulty and ultimately destroyed the Japanese naval air force. The Americans brought people home from combat regions after a relatively short time to become instructors, and thus pass along their knowledge. But the Japanese kept their first-class pilots in the front line, until they were killed. This happened time and again throughout the war. Only a handful of the many aces of Japan survived. The best of the naval pilots manned the planes of the Nagumo force. Lately the Japanese lost about 250 planes, but they also lost nearly that many pilots from the four carriers.

They should have learned from the battle of the Coral Sea, in which so many pilots were lost that the carrier *Zuikaku* could not muster enough pilots to let her come on the Midway mission. After Midway the cream of the Japanese naval air force was lost, and it was never the same again.

And finally, a major reason for the resounding defeat of the Japanese at Midway was the arrogance of the "victory disease." When planning the operation, a spokesman for the naval general staff made a most ridiculous observation:

> What we are most concerned with in this operation is the enemy will be loath to meet our fleet, and will refuse to come out from his base.

The height of the arrogance was displayed by no less a personage than the chief of staff to the chief of the Combined Fleet. Admiral Matome Ugaki took it upon himself to rearrange the results of the war games at which the Midway plan was being tested.

Here is what Fuchida and Okumiya have to say on that subject:

> When, following the established rule for the games, nine enemy hits were scored and two Japanese carriers sunk thereby, these results were arbitrarily reduced, first to only three hits scored, sinking one carrier and damaging another, and finally to no carriers lost at all. The same flexible system of calculation was employed to establish plane losses, highly favorable, of course, to the Japanese.

Had the plan been surveyed more critically it might have been changed, and if it had been changed, Japan might not have lost all those four carriers after all.

But it happened, and Japan, which went into the battle of Midway with what appeared to be overwhelming power, lost the battle and her naval power was never again the same. And yet as will be seen, the loss at Midway did not put an end to the "Victory disease." It would continue and would again cost the Japanese dear.

CHAPTER FIFTEEN

The Aleutians

In 1941 the almost uninhabitable Aleutian Islands were inhabited only by American army and navy establishments at Dutch Harbor; there were a few houses there, and a small settlement of the native population on Attu and Atka Islands.

When the Americans learned that the Japanese contemplated invading these islands they found it difficult to understand why, although the army's General Billy Mitchell, the advocate of air power, had predicted earlier that this would be the Japanese route. One very real reason that the Japanese wanted the Aleutian bases was to prevent the Americans from launching air attacks on Japan from here. After the Doolittle raid on Japan, this was a real threat to the Japanese. They knew the Americans had begun building "super-fortresses," with bigger and better bombing capabilities than those of the B-17 bomber, and that their announced purpose was to bomb Japan. Since the 1930s the Japanese warlords had been cognizant of the vulnerability of the wood-and-paper Japanese cities and they had an enormous fear of the possibility of bombing.

In a sense the whole Aleutians campaign was a comedy of errors and misplaced intelligence. The Japanese feared that the Americans were massing troops on the West Coast, and that they would carry out an invasion of Japan from the Aleutians. One way to stop that was to put bases in the Aleutians from which they could watch and prevent American bombing raids as well.

The Americans, on the other side, were very much afraid that the Japanese were planning to invade the West Coast of the United States, and principal among the high-ranking people who shared this fear was Admiral King, who insisted that the American battleship fleet be concentrated on the West Coast to resist the invasion he half-expected.

The American navy had built airfields at Kiska, at Dutch Harbor, and at Kodiak. The army had also built staging air bases from Puget Sound, Washington, up to the Alaska Peninsula. These bases were manned by the XI Army Air Force.

Alaska was defended by army and navy. The army command was the Alaskan Defense Command headed by Brigadier General Simon Bolivar Buckner. The navy command was the Alaskan Sector of the Thirteenth Naval District at Seattle. Captain Ralph C. Parker was the navy commander, and his command was the gunboat *Charleston*. He also had three patrol boats which were converted fishing boats. By the spring of 1942 the Alaska navy had been augmented to a total of two old destroyers, two coast guard cutters, more fishing boat converts and then PBY flying boats.

When the American naval radio intelligence intercepts revealed that the Japanese were planning an invasion of the Aleutians as part of their Midway plan, Admiral Nimitz upgraded the Alaskan defense by sending Rear Admiral Robert A. Theobald to the Alaskan area, along with five cruisers, 14 destroyers, and six submarines. Ultimately this became known as the North Pacific Force.

The Americans knew the Japanese were coming, but they did not know a great deal more than that in the first days of June 1942.

The Japanese had entrusted the invasion of the Aleutians to Vice Admiral Yoshiro Hosogaya, the commander of the Fifth Fleet. His flagship was the cruiser *Nachi*. He had three cruisers and two light cruisers, two light carriers, a handful of destroyers, transports for the troops who would occupy the islands, a seaplane carrier, a few support ships, and six submarines.

Early in June Admiral Nimitz had finally puzzled out the Japanese intentions and saw that they did not involve any major activity but only landings at Attu and Kiska. Admiral Theobald did not believe this, and thought the Japanese would try a more extensive operation, perhaps by taking Dutch Harbor. The Japanese had in fact considered this but rejected the idea because they believed Dutch Harbor was defended by the whole army division, which was not true. Admiral Theobald was very much worried because he did not feel that he had the air might to counter the two Japanese light carriers that were coming. The army planes available were unsuitable, and the flying boats were useful for patrol and search and bombing, but that was about all.

When Admiral Theobald arrived, he persuaded the army to move its planes around to the western bases at Cold Bay and Otter Point. Twenty-one P-40s and 14 bombers were flown up to Cold Bay and 12 P-40s to Otter Point. The planes had radar but the pilots had no experience in flying over water and no experience in Alaska.

On June 1 Admiral Theobald left Kodiak in the cruiser and headed south to meet the rest of his fleet. He had guessed incorrectly that the Japanese would land near Dutch Harbor, so his fleet was out of the action, 400 miles to the south. In fact, Admiral Kakuta, the commander of the two Japanese light carriers, had already made his air strike before Admiral Theobald joined up with his ships.

The Japanese Northern Force had been organized at Minato, on the north of Honshu Island, and trained there and on Hokkaido for the amphibious landings in the Aleutians. The carrier force left Japan on May 25 and by the 28th all the ships were at sea, except the supply units and the flagship, for Admiral Hosogaya came with the supply ships and did not sail until June 2. On the morning of June 3, Admiral Kakuta's strike force of planes hit Dutch Harbor but did not do it very well, for the planes of the *Junyo* turned back in bad weather. The *Ryujo*'s attack group did better; it bombed and strafed Dutch Harbor for 20 minutes and did considerable damage and killed 25 soldiers and sailors. One plane was shot down by the Americans. The Japanese also spotted five destroyers in Makushin Bay and Admiral Kakuta sent his second strike against the destroyers, but the weather closed in and the planes could not find any destroyers. When part of the force flew over Otter Point on Umnak Island two P-40s shot down two Japanese planes and seriously damaged two more. The Otter Point airfield was concealed by overcast, but the American planes used radar and the Japanese could not figure out where they came from.

The Japanese then retired to the southwest. They were sighted by a PBY flying through the murk and fog, but no accurate fix was made on the Japanese force.

Admiral Theobald, who had a bad temper anyhow, grew very restless and angry because he could not find his enemies. So he left the main body and headed for Kodiak.

Admiral Kakuta fueled and then, as ordered, attacked Adak, or tried to. Morning of June 4 brought a fog so thick that speed had to be cut to nine knots, and his weathermen predicted the weather around Adak would be terrible but that around Dutch Harbor would be good. So Kakuta decided to attack Dutch Harbor again.

The weather was so bad that all the American search planes and picket boats missed the Japanese planes, and at four o'clock on the afternoon of June 4, while the battle was raging at Midway, the *Ryujo* and the *Junyo* launched their planes, 17 bombers and 15 fighters. They took off, and then the American search planes finally spooked the task force and bombers were sent out, but it was a case of groping through the fog, and when they did find the carriers, the conditions for bombing were terrible and they got no hits at all but a couple of near-misses. A B-26 medium bomber and a B-17 were shot down over the carriers.

The lucky Japanese planes found fine weather at Dutch Harbor and destroyed four big new fuel tanks, part of a hospital, an uncompleted hangar, and the beached ship *Northwestern*.

On their way back to the carriers, the Japanese planes saw for the first time the American airfield at Otter Point. Up came the P-40s again and shot down three of the *Junyo* planes. The Americans had also suffered from attrition, largely due to weather. Six PBYs, three bombers, and two P-40 fighters had been lost.

As his planes were coming home, Admiral Kakuta was learning of the disaster that had befallen Admiral Nagumo at Midway, and was receiving orders to hurry south and help out. The occupation of the Aleutians was to be postponed temporarily. But soon enough Yamamoto learned that it was no use, and there was no hope of making a strike back at the Americans because Kakuta could not arrive in time to affect the outcome of the battle. So the temporary restraint on the Aleutians landings was removed and the Japanese up north were told to go ahead and follow their original plan.

So Kakuta turned north again, and met Admiral Hosogaya. The Japanese milled around the Aleutians in the bad weather, and did not do very much. Actually it was very hard for anybody to accomplish much in the way of warfare in this climate, in this season, with the constant light, and the constant bad weather.

Captain Parker was very much concerned about the continuing losses of his PBYs to weather and he complained to Admiral Nimitz that he needed more planes, and Nimitz promised to comply, but it would be a few days before the planes would arrive.

Meanwhile the Japanese were moving to occupy Attu and Kiska. They were also planning to attack Adak, but when they learned of the air base at Umnak which had cost them several planes already, Admiral Hosogaya decided against it. So the Japanese moved against Attu. On the morning of June 7 they landed 1,200 troops at Attu, in thick fog. They landed at Holtz Bay, and marched overland through snow to Chichagof. The main force got lost, but that was not too important, because when the others got to Chichagof ready to assault all the soldiers there, they found 39 Aleutian natives, 15 of them children, and Mr. and Mrs. Charles Jones, missionaries. The Japanese took all of them prisoner. Then they proceeded to unload their equipment and settle down in this unfriendly atmosphere for an occupation.

The Kiska occupation force was led in by the seaplane carrier on June 7 as well, without opposition from the only Americans there, then members of a weather team. The Japanese were ready for a fight but there was nobody to fight.

But when it was all done and won, how irrelevant it had become, made so by the failure at Midway. For among other things, the Aleutians bases were to be the northern anchor of a new Japanese defense line, running from the Aleutians to Midway and then to the inner empire. The Aleutians were to be supplied from the new Midway base. But now there was no Midway, there was no new defense line. The Aleutians would have to be supplied from Japan, and it had all become a nuisance. Still, Imperial General Headquarters decided to hang on for reasons of face, and for whatever nuisance value the Aleutians bases might offer, and in keeping with the original plan of preventing the Americans from using the Aleutians as bases of their new B-29 bombers which would soon be ready.

So the Japanese occupation began. The Americans tried to find the Japanese ships, but failed in the bad weather. There were several false starts and spurts of activity; at one point Admiral Nimitz thought the Japanese were operating two or three major carriers in the north, but he was soon disabused of all this, and the Americans and the Japanese settled down to see how they could fight each other in the execrable climate. On June 10, one of the PBYs, fighting fog again, found the Japanese camp on Kiska, and reported on four ships, and then the tent colony on Attu Island. When Admiral Nimitz learned of this, he ordered the submarines to move in and begin working this area, and also the air forces to bomb the Japanese. The PBYs tried to take on the job. For two days they bombed, and the army bombers bombed, but none of the attacks was very successful. Weather again. The Japanese also undertook some air activity. They had moved seaplanes and flying boats up to Kiska from Japan, and they attacked some American installations. But the Americans scored the first real success, bombing and sinking the Japanese transport *Nissan Maru*, off Kiska on June 18.

After that the Americans and the Japanese settled down to what turned out to be a long campaign of attrition.

CHAPTER SIXTEEN

Troubles at Home

Summer 1942. At home in Japan the euphoria continued: victory, victory, victory. Outside the general staff, no one knew what had happened at Midway; it was heralded by the Imperial General Staff spokesman as a victory, with great emphasis being put on the Aleutians landings as if they were the raison d'être for the whole enterprise. But in the shipyards, where the naval ships were under construction, they knew already.

Between 1919 and 1941 the Mitsubishi and Kawasaki companies had built 23 cruisers for the Japanese navy, ranging in size from the 5,000-ton *Sendai* to the 13,000-ton *Takao*. After 1937 five passenger liners were converted to be aircraft carriers. In 1939 Kawasaki built the *Zuikaku* and the *Shokaku* with hangar space for 84 planes, and in 1940 Mitsubishi launched the *Musashi*, the sister battleship of the *Yamato*, which had joined the fleet a year earlier.

By Pearl Harbor Day the Japanese had the most powerful battle fleet in the world. And now, in midsummer 1942, they still did have. But four of the mighty carriers had been lost and there was no way, the shipbuilders knew, to replace them. Japan simply did not have the steel, the coal, the copper, and the other materials needed. Moreover, the shortage of merchant shipping was already so great that military expansion had been delayed, and supply of such distant bastions as Rabaul was so difficult that the army opted to concentrate supplies there for the whole South Pacific area for more than a year.

The Ministry of Communications, which was in charge of the shipbuilding program, could not build ships fast enough to serve this new empire which sprawled over a third of the globe.

Recognizing this, in the summer of 1942 Prime Minister Tōjō gave the navy the responsibility for ship production, in the hope that the desperate situation could be remedied.

They took a page straight out of the American book. In 1941, sensing the coming crisis, Henry Kaiser, at shipyards in California and Oregon, had pioneered a new sort of ship-building, with the use of welded steel plates instead of riveted parts. Soon the Americans were building 10,000-ton freighters in a matter of days. The record was four days, 15.5 hours.

But the Japanese ship production under the navy was already improving. To do that, however, the Japanese yards had to concentrate on merchant shipping. American shipyards were now building small carriers for escort service, again in a matter of weeks and days. But not the Japanese. They were already discovering that their war effort and expansion was greater than they could support. All work on battleships was abandoned once the *Musashi* was launched. The carrier *Shinano* was still under construction, but the work already lagged because of shortages of materials. After Midway, orders for six new carriers were placed, but these would have to be smaller for the most part.

So Japan in 1942 was building six carriers, no battleships, and three cruisers. Meanwhile the U.S. was building three battleships, 34 carriers, and 10 cruisers.

Aircraft were, of course, vital to the war, and army and navy vied for shares of industrial production. By 1941 the Japanese aircraft industry was concentrated in a number of large factories around Nagoya, Tokyo, Osaka, and Kobe. Parts were farmed out to cottage industries in these cities. Japan's aircraft production seemed to be satisfactory—8;900 planes produced in 1942—but that same year the Americans produced 49,000 aircraft.

Since 1937 the Japanese coal industry had been working to reach production of 70 million tons by 1942. This summer it was obvious they were not going to achieve this goal; coal production was leveling off at 54 million tons, not enough to feed the ever more demanding war effort. The problem of shortage of labor had already surfaced, with 100,000 miners sent to the armed services. After the fall of Singapore and the investment of the Dutch East Indies, Prime Minister Tōjō had decreed that war prisoners were going to be made to earn their keep in places like the mines. The coal for the iron and steel industry was imported from Manchuria, but that meant either more ships or more trains, and both were in short supply.

Just after the battle, a disaster had struck the important colliery at Honkeiko in Manchukuo. On April 26 a typhoon had cut the electric power lines that served the mine, one of the largest in the world. The underground ventilation suddenly stopped, turned off by the men on the surface. But no one told the pit crews what had happened. A conveyor belt operator wondered what had happened to his equipment. He started to remove a switch and suddenly, again without notice, the surface crew turned the power back on. The wire to the conveyor belt short-circuited and ignited a concentration of methane gas and coal dust that had built up when the ventilation system was turned off. On the surface, a steel frame building above the pit entrance was obliterated, so powerful was the blast. Rescue teams were sent down, but the concentration of gas and smoke was too much for them and they retreated to the surface. A few miners managed to crawl to the surface but the vast majority were injured or killed—268 injured and 1,527 killed. Production at this important mine was completely shut down for 30 days. Of course the disaster was concealed from the Japanese public by government censorship, but the men in the steel mills and the shipyards and the aircraft factories knew that they were not receiving their supplies.

Although maintaining adequate food supplies had not yet been a serious problem in Japan, and the situation promised to be improved with the acquisition of rice-growing areas in Indochina, the Dutch East Indies, and Malaysia, there were signs already of shortages. In 1937 the Japanese economy had been put on a war footing, and the government controlled distribution of foodstuffs. In 1941 Tōjō announced that Japan would have to become self-sufficient in food production, and all areas of agriculture were put under government control.

But farm production, having hit a high in 1939, was already decreasing as the number of farm workers went down. Once again the reason was the demand of the army and navy for manpower.

During the war years the labor force in the agricultural sector would decrease by five million men, most of them young and middle-aged. Already in 1942 the farm sector was feeling the pinch caused by Japan's reckless ambition to dominate Asia and the Pacific.

The motor vehicle industry of Japan was also feeling the pinch. Already gasoline was virtually nonexistent in the civil sector. Since the 1930s the Japanese had been occupying ever larger areas of China, and there was an enormous, insatiable demand for armored cars, trucks, artillery tractors, tanks, and general utility vehicles and staff cars. In the 1920s the Americans had pioneered in the Japanese market; Ford, Chevrolet, and General Motors set up assembly lines and in 1929 they produced 30,000 cars in Japan. But when the army took power, the first thing they did was begin the elimination of foreign vehicles. The army even then was looking toward a general war and saw that Japan must be self-sufficient. By 1938 production had expanded so rapidly that foreign import was stopped altogether. In 1941 the industry produced 48,000 cars and trucks, and built more than 1,000 tanks. By 1942 the Japanese army had 62,000 trucks in service, and was calling for more. Transport in China and throughout the new empire was in very short supply.

Gasoline rationing, which began for civilians, started in 1938. By 1942 only a conniver or an official had a car. There were no tires, the production of buses stopped, taxicabs disappeared from the streets, and the cars that ran were powered by charcoal and could only chug along. But the demands were impossible, the supplies of metal and parts were failing, and the production of trucks began to decline in this summer of 1942. By enforcing stringent economy measures, the army maintained production of tanks. At the moment the Japanese could not conceive of heavy losses—they had won everywhere but on the sea—but as time went on, they would lose more than 70,000 trucks overseas to bombing and fighting.

In the summer of 1942 the Japanese still believed they had forever solved their petroleum problem with the capture of the East Indian oil fields. They had stockpiled oil in those years before the U.S. embargoed the product to Japan, but by December 1941 their stocks had fallen from 51 million barrels to 43 million barrels. The government had begun a synthetic oil production program in 1937 with the aim of producing 14 million barrels a year. But this year only 1.5 million barrels would be produced, an enormous disappointment. The problem was again a shortage of manpower, a shortage of technicians, a shortage of steel, and a shortage of coal. And just now they were leaning on the technology of their partner in war, Germany, for a synthetic plant built by the Germans to employ the Fischer-Tropf process of synthetic oil production.

The Germans also sent technicians to Japan to assist at the Omuta Works. But the Japanese could not provide the high-quality coal that was needed for the process, and their production line suffered from lack of maintenance. They never achieved more than one-third of the production they had expected.

This summer the real problems would begin. The plant was supposed to produce significant quantities of oil, but because the electrical system kept breaking down due to lack of maintenance, the plant never produced more than a few hundred barrels a day.

The Japanese were learning that the Sumatran and Borneo oil fields produced a crude oil with a high sulfur content, ruinous to ships' boiler systems.

The textile industry had been one of peacetime Japan's strongest and she had successfully challenged the major producers of the world. But when Japan decided on war and conquest, emphasis was placed on the heavy industries and the textile industry began to falter. After 1941 millions of metal textile spindles were melted down to make munitions. Mills were converted to making chemicals or airplane parts and the dye industry was converted to making explosives. Almost all foreign markets were cut off by the war; exports fell by 98 percent, and even domestic production suffered. By 1942 people were feeling the effects of shortages of clothing, and advertisements appeared in the newspapers to trade clothes for various other items. The newspaper classified advertising column became a sort of barter medium; almost anything useful was worth trading for something you needed, because virtually every consumer product was in short supply.

Had the Japanese military oligarchy possessed any real sense of economics, they would never have indulged in war with the Western powers. The Japanese steel industry had always depended on imported raw materials. For years the Japanese had bought all the scrap steel the Americans could provide, and suddenly in 1941 all this was cut off as a result of the Japanese march into Indochina. When war came the generals believed they could rely on the production capacity of their steel industry and raw materials from Manchuria and China. But the Chinese were hardly cooperative and Manchuria could not provide all that was needed. As the war went on, transportation of ores became an enormous problem, and already the American submarine force was cutting into shipments. By 1942 the airplane industry was beginning to feel the steel shortage too, and plain steel was substituted for special steel alloys, sometimes with disastrous results. Because of the shortage of steel for mining equipment, accidents and problems in coal mines increased six-fold in the years 1941 and 1942.

Iron and steel making was carried out in four main areas: the *Kamaishi Muroran,* in north Japan; the Tokyo area; the Osaka-Kobe area; and in northern Kyushu. The biggest plant was the government plant at Yawata on Kyushu. Almost half Japan's steel and a quarter of its pig iron was produced here. The ores came from the local Chikuho field and from north China. Steel from Yawata was used for guns and shell cases in the Kokura army arsenal and for warships built in the Ubishi shipyards at Nagasaki. But by 1942 production was already endangered by lack of supplies of raw materials—and the bombing of Japan had not even yet begun.

So by 1942 Japanese industry was already in deep trouble.

It took a Japanese chemical works a thousand man-hours to produce a ton of smokeless powder, while it took the Americans only five man-hours to do the same. Nearly half of all the aluminum delivered to industry was defective or spoiled on the assembly lines, and had to be scrapped; it was then sold on the black market where everything was for sale.

Steel plates delivered to industry began to crack, due to inferior materials. Gun barrels, made with steel containing too much phosphorus, tended to explode after a number of rounds had been fired. The steel in aircraft caused problems; some Nakajima K184 fighter planes collapsed because the engine was too heavy for the frail landing gear.

The army and the navy were already quarreling over allocation of almost everything. The navy was given responsibility for air protection of all the far-flung empire outposts, but got only half the planes put out by industry. Increasingly, this allocation became harder for the naval forces to bear and was a major point of friction between army and navy, but since Prime Minister Tōjō was an army man there was nothing to be done.

Every year since 1937 the strictures of mobilization for total war had intensified. The thought-control laws were strengthened, the censorship of the press was tightened, the propaganda barrage against the Japanese people was never-ending. Every day they were reminded that this was total war and they had an important part in it. On the 8th day of every month every newspaper carried the Imperial Rescript announcing the war on the front page. Every time a new victory or an apparent victory or even a pretend victory was achieved, a new Imperial Rescript was issued in praise of the troops and navy. Thus already were sown the seeds of substitution: each physical shortage was to be met by belt-tightening and the cry of the government that Japan's superior morality and strength of character would win out against the gathering odds.

CHAPTER SEVENTEEN

Remnants and Rovers

On the day that President Roosevelt declared war on Japan, following the Pearl Harbor attack, Admiral Stark, the chief of naval operations, ordered unrestricted submarine warfare against Japan, and within a few days the submarines began to set out from Pearl Harbor. From the very first, the Americans followed a German tactic and used the submarines to attack Japan's lifeline of freighters and tankers which brought in the supplies that let her carry on the war. The Japanese, on the other hand, followed the traditional use of submarines, as eyes of the fleet and attack weapons against other warships. The Germans in two wars had used the submarines as commerce destroyers, but were roundly criticized for this practice internationally after World War I. When World War II came, all the fine talk about use of submarines under controlled conditions vanished very quickly. From the beginning of the European sea war, when the liner *Athenia* was sunk without warning in the Atlantic, the first lord of the British admiralty, Winston Churchill, declared outright warfare against submarines. In violation of agreements he armed the British steamers, and in very short order all the good intentions of the 'tween-wars period had given way to sinking without notice by submarines, along with ruthless depth-charging and abandonment of survivors of sunk submarines by the Allies. It was not a nice war, from the outset, and the Americans plunged into it in the Pacific as a very grim business indeed.

On the day that Admiral Chester W. Nimitz arrived at Pearl Harbor and took command of the U.S. Pacific Fleet, he flew his flag aboard the submarine *Grayling,* and from that time onward the flagship of the fleet was a submarine. This went back to Nimitz's own experience as a young submarine officer in the Philippines during the Philippine insurrection.

It was not long after the disastrous battle of the Java Sea that the American submarine *Trout* made her third war patrol and penetrated deep into the waters of Japan, just off the Honshu coast. On April 9, 1942, her skipper sighted two small freighters making their way along the coast to Kobe. These were the first Japanese ships he had seen for a long time, and although they were sm... he decided to have a go at them. But he could not get within a mile of them because of currents and coastline. The next day, however, Lieutenant Commander Frank W. Fenno saw a long column of smoke and followed it until he came to a steamer. He did not want to waste torpedoes so he fired one torpedo, but it did not connect. Then he fired another. Same result. Then up came an escort and chased the submarine, as did the steamer, and the Americans thought they had gotten into trouble with a Q-ship, a ship designed to lure submarines and then help sink them. So after hours of playing mouse to the Japanese cat, the *Trout* escaped and went her way.

It was disappointing to lose three ships, but soon a 25,000-ton ship, quite a big one, came along very close to the Honshu coast, so close that her camouflaged decks blended in with the cliffs. Fenno fired two torpedoes from a mile off, and one of them connected. The ship stopped and it seemed she was hard-hit. But the crew got the engines started again, and the ship escaped toward the sea. Fenno chased her but he could not surface because he was right under a Japanese shore battery. So the ship, much faster on the surface than the submarine below, escaped to sea. Fenno got close enough to try one more torpedo but the profile of the ship was so narrow that it missed.

The torpedoes' misses were probably caused by flaws in either the magnetic exploder warhead, copied from the Germans after World War I, or the depth control. American torpedoes for the first year and a half of the war had lots of problems, and these two features were among the worst. Many a skipper fired at a ship only to see nothing happen, which meant that the torpedo had gone underneath the hull, defying his attempts to set a proper depth. More frustrating and more common was when a torpedo hit square and nothing happened. That was when the exploder failed, and a ship that should have been sunk got away.

Skipper Fenno was ready to go for more game, but he had a message from Pearl Harbor that he was to move out to the southwest. Admiral Halsey and the *Enterprise* and the *Hornet* were bringing a contingent of B-25 medium army bombers to stage an attack on Japan, and they needed all the help they could get. The *Trout* was detailed to cover the approach of the carriers, give weather warnings, and check for Japanese naval ship activity. So she was occupied for more than a week, and did not get back to the Honshu coast until April 23. This time she ran into a part of the Japanese fishing fleet, which combed the waters 20 to 30 miles offshore. Perhaps 20 or 30 boats from one fishing town went out each day, and they stayed quite close together. The *Trout* was in the middle of them, and she surfaced this night to find a long line and a glass float tangled around her conning tower. What the Japanese net fishermen thought had happened to their line and float was never known.

On April 24 the *Trout* found a 10,000-ton Japanese tanker, a ship the size of an American liberty ship; but she did not sink her although she fired two torpedoes. The tanker was stopped for a while, and then a small freighter came up.

The *Trout* sank her with two more torpedoes, one of which worked, and then Fenno hauled out, because he was moving in close to shore, and the Japanese antisubmarine defenses were alerted.

After the battle of the Java Sea, the remnants of the United States Asiatic Fleet moved from the Philippines and the Dutch East Indies down to Australia.

So on April 1 they were beginning their patrols, from Fremantle, near Perth, and from Brisbane on the north coast of Australia. Captain John Wilkes, who had come down from Manila by way of the Dutch Islands, was in command of these submarines, mostly old-fashioned S-boats.

On April 27 the *Trout* sank a Japanese patrol boat, which might have been called the waste of a torpedo, but in the early days of the war anything that meant trouble for the enemy was acceptable. Then he fired three torpedoes at two merchant ships and got no hits. The torpedoes passed under the ships. On May 2 the same thing happened when he fired at a passenger vessel. But then Fenno found a 5,000-ton freighter and sank her with one torpedo. On May 4 he sank another patrol boat.

The Japanese were looking for him, and the *Trout* was subjected to a series of bombings by aircraft, but none of the depth charges connected. By this time the *Trout* had been out for more than 40 days and had fired 22 of her 24 torpedoes. It would take them several weeks to get home so their patrol turned out to be longer than the average 47 days. But it was also more successful because Fenno had sunk three ships and damaged two others.

The Pacific Fleet submarine commander, Rear Admiral Robert English, had imposed a ban on the firing of spreads of torpedoes, in order to conserve torpedoes. But the submariners of this day were a trigger-happy lot. In mid-April, on the way out to patrol in the East China Sea, the *Triton* spotted a Japanese fishing boat, a trawler. It was hardly a major target, but Lieutenant Commander Charles C. Kirkpatrick fired two torpedoes at her, which missed the vessel, and then the *Triton* came to the surface and used her three-inch deck gun and 50-caliber machine guns to wreck the trawler.

Near the end of April, the *Triton* entered the East China Sea, and after seeing nothing for three days, found a convoy. The skipper tracked the convoy and fired two torpedoes, but missed. He tried again and this second time one of the two torpedoes damaged the 5,000-ton freighter *Calcutta Maru*. The convoy escorts came to depth-charge, but the *Triton* submerged and got out of the way. Later in the day, Skipper Kirkpatrick brought the *Triton* back for another shot at the *Calcutta Maru*. This time she sank.

The next action came when the submarine encountered another convoy on May 6. The *Triton* then ran from the escorts. On May 15 the *Triton* attacked two Japanese fishing boats,

sank one easily, and then boarded the second, took off enough
fish for dinner, and then put the crew into boats and sank the
ship.

Off Japan the *Triton* got sight of a carrier but was unable
to close with her. Cruising off Kyushu, she saw the Japanese
submarine *I-164* on the surface, took a shot with a torpedo,
and blew up the submarine. On June 21 the *Triton* fired four
torpedoes at another submarine on the surface but did not score
any hits. Her patrol, too, was coming to an end and she returned
to Pearl Harbor. Other patrols from Pearl Harbor that spring
were not quite so successful.

But two could play the torpedo game, and the *Thresher*, in
early April, was nearly torpedoed by an unseen Japanese submarine. The *Thresher* had torpedo problems, too, and missed
a large merchantman, but hit a 3,000-ton freighter. Overall she
was not very lucky on this trip. She was on the surface one
day when a freak wave pooped her—that is, washed water
down the open hatches—and this water disrupted the electrical
system and caused great damage, so much in fact that the boat
had to end her patrol and go back to Pearl Harbor with only
one vessel sunk and most of her torpedoes still aboard.

The Japanese had some large ships, too, and they were used
in convoys to Saigon, Hong Kong, and other southern ports
which were now part of the Japanese empire. South of Kyushu
one day in May, the submarine *Grenadier* came across a convoy and tracked it, and fired two torpedoes at a large ship. She
sank the *Taiyo Maru*.

By the spring of 1942 the torpedo situation had improved
at Pearl Harbor at least in numbers, and some skippers were
firing spreads. It was fine when it worked, but when it did not,
as with the *Drum* off the coast of Kyushu when she fired at a
large transport, then it was sheer waste.

But one can imagine the frustration of a submarine captain
who journeyed across the Pacific and then saw nothing; it was
this frustration that caused the skipper of *Pompano* to waste a
torpedo on a sampan off the China coast. Much better was her
sinking of a small tanker, and then a large transport.

During June many of the American submarines at Pearl Harbor were involved in the Midway operation, hunting for the enemy fleet. Twelve boats patrolled off Midway, three halfway between Midway and Oahu, and three guarded Oahu, which might possibly have been the point of attack. As it turned out none of the American submarines really got into the action except the *Nautilus,* which got one shot at a battleship but missed, and put a dud torpedo into the *Kaga,* and put three torpedoes into the damaged *Soryu,* thus hastening her end.

Two American submarines went into the Marshall Islands and the Admiralties and brought home photographs of the Japanese installations on Eniwetok in the Marshalls and the big naval base at Truk.

What was needed in the spring of 1942 was a coordinated attack. The Pearl Harbor submarines until Midway had been shooting out, hither and thither, but from the reports the boats brought back, a pattern began to emerge, showing that the major traffic of importance ran between the Indies and Saigon, Taiwan, and then the Japanese islands. So the Japanese islands began to get more attention from the American submarine force. The first target, Number One as the Japanese would say, was the entrance to Tokyo Bay, from which ships and warships traveled to Tokyo, Yokohama, and the big naval base. American submarines also found good hunting outside the entrances to the Inland Sea, although they did not then dare go into that fiercely guarded water.

After the safety of Midway Island was assured by the victory at sea, the atoll was developed into a major submarine staging base, and all boats that set out for Japanese waters refueled there.

American submarines that summer of 1942 began moving father and farther into Japanese waters. The *Guardfish* traveled to the waters off northeast Honshu in August, and sank two small vessels and then a 3,000-ton passenger liner operating between Hokkaido and the main island. Her main triumph on this patrol was to sink two ships in one convoy on September 4. That same day she sank another two ships, all of this action taken near Kuji Bay.

By the middle of the summer in 1942 the operational officers of the fleet were largely convinced that something was wrong with the American torpedoes, and at Pearl Harbor Admiral English made some changes.

In Australia Captain Wilkes was harder to convince. Skippers would come in to Darwin or Brisbane with stories of torpedoes that did not explode, and his tendency was to blame the captain or the torpedo officer for error. The reason: Captain Wilkes had been instrumental in the development of this torpedo and the firing mechanism, and he had confidence in it. But by midsummer most of the submarine captains had lost their confidence in the quality of the torpedoes; all of them had bad experiences to report.

From London, Rear Admiral Charles Lockwood was dispatched to command the submarine force in Western Australia and set up his headquarters near Fremantle. He quickly became convinced that the captains were right, and he, too, gave permission for the skippers to use contact explosion, rather than the magnetic exploder device that seemed to cause so much trouble. Immediately the score of his submarines began to rise.

In the springtime and increasingly during the summer, submarines made the run from Pearl Harbor to Japanese waters and then down to Australia as the Australia force, largely consisting of old S-boats, was augmented with some new fleet-class submarines. Commander J. H. Willingham took the *Tautog* on this route, and on the way sank two Japanese submarines and a 4,000-ton freighter. The *Stingray* was another boat that made the run several times, and also traveled through the Gilbert and Marshall Islands. The *Thresher* had a strange escape in the Marshalls. She had attacked a ship and then submerged. Suddenly strange clanking noises were heard, and the submarine found herself hooked by a huge grapnel, towed by the Japanese, and apparently about to be reeled in like a giant fish. Her skipper backed and filled and finally broke the grapnel loose. Then the Japanese began depth-charging, but the *Thresher* escaped and arrived off Truk, and then moved into Java waters and finally safely into Fremantle Harbor.

* * *

Down in the South Pacific the submarines and a half a dozen old destroyers comprised what came to be known as MacArthur's navy. Just after the debacle in Java, the submarines had a lot of work to do to evacuate agents and refugee troops from areas recently occupied by the Japanese. They also very soon began to make contact with the American and Filipino troops left on the southern Philippine Islands, who had elected to fight guerilla warfare against the Japanese. Indeed, throughout the rest of the war, these forces were assisted and supplied from Australia by submarine.

Soon the submarine force in Australia was split, and MacArthur got part of them at Brisbane under Captain James Fife, while the boats under Captain Ralph Christie at Fremantle were operating with the Pacific Fleet. This led to a good deal of conflict within the American naval organization, but MacArthur did not send submarines up north, and the patrol of the mandates was best carried out in conjunction with activity at Fremantle.

In the spring, Captain Wilkes had 231 fleet boats and five S-boats. Six more S-boats were sent out for Brisbane, and the five S-boats at Fremantle were sent up and Task Force Forty-two was organized under Rear Admiral Francis Rockwell. Later Captain Christie replaced him.

Some of the first missions of the *Sturgeon* and the *Spearfish* were to go to the Dutch East Indies and evacuate Allied personnel who had been stranded there by the rapid advance of the Japanese. The *Spearfish* went to the Philippines, where she evacuated army and navy nurses from Corregidor; that was in April, a few weeks before the surrender. The *Seawolf* operated off Java, where she attacked a Japanese light cruiser. The *Searaven* evacuated a number of Australians from Timor; the *Porpoise* rescued five downed army fliers from an island near Halmahera.

These were not the usual missions for which submarines had been devised, but they were all essential in the wake of this enormously speedy Japanese advance down into the South Pacific.

* * *

The *Salmon* sank a Japanese repair ship near Lombok Strait, and soon in that same general region sank another ship at the end of May. The *Skipjack* sailed into Camranh Bay, the Japanese naval base in Indochina. She sank several ships, lost several because of faulty torpedoes, and the skipper joined the growing number of complainers about the torpedoes. This had been going on since the Philippines, and the most experienced skippers were the ones who complained the most bitterly. In fact, at about this same time the Germans were just starting with new torpedoes, having learned themselves during the battle for Norway that their exploders were faulty. But it was taking the Americans more time, because the experts of the Bureau of Ordnance simply would not accept the reports from the men in the field and continued to believe all this was alibi by incompetent submarine captains.

Captain Fife grew so annoyed with all this up at Brisbane that he had a skipper fire torpedoes against a net, and proved to his own satisfaction that the torpedoes were running 10 feet deeper than the settings. The word was passed to Admiral King, and finally he was sufficiently convinced to order the Bureau of Ordnance to check its findings. Then the bureau for the first time paid attention, and in a few weeks, reported that the torpedoes did indeed run 10 feet deep. How many *Maru*s had escaped while the experts were fiddling? No one wanted to count.

The problem of the firing mechanism remained. Captain Christie was one of the last to concede that there was anything wrong with the firing arrangement, because he had been one of the designers of the exploder. But because of that, Christie was brought back to Washington to work with the Bureau of Ordnance, and Rear Admiral Lockwood took over. He was much more receptive to the complaints of his captains, and he immediately began making tests. They were not quite that conclusive, but the skippers knew. They knew!

The biggest problem of the Southwest Pacific submarines was that of getting any torpedoes at all. So many had been abandoned in the Philippines surrender that the Australia station was in short supply for more than a year. Pearl Harbor was also short, but somehow because it was Fleet Headquarters, it managed. But many submarine captains in the Southwest Pacific would go out with half a load of torpedoes and instructions to make every shot count. It was hard to do when about half the time the firing pin did not work right.

Following the capture of the Netherlands East Indies the Japanese timetable of conquest had to be revised because it had all been so easy and so fast. That is why the attempt to capture Port Moresby was put together in such a hurry, and why the Japanese moved to support the other landings in Lae and Salamaua without proper preparation.

There was nothing in the spring of 1942 that could stop them from expanding. Their base at Rabaul was the most powerful bastion in the South Pacific.

The Allies had so few warships in the South Pacific that they hesitated to risk them in open opposition to the Japanese operations around New Guinea. Therefore, the only restraining influences were Allied air power and submarine power. Allied air power was in a formative period; Lieutenant General George C. Kenney's Fifth Air Force was just being built up with medium and heavy bombers from the United States. So the submarines at this point were extremely important in the Allied plans.

That summer the submarine zones of operation were split up. The MacArthur command at Brisbane had control of the Australian-mandated territory, which included the Solomon Islands and New Guinea. The Central Pacific submarines at Pearl Harbor were assigned to work the East China Sea north of the Philippines, the Western Pacific as far as Palau, and the area around Taiwan. The South Pacific boats under Admiral Lockwood patrolled the Philippines and the Indies. Early patrols from Fremantle were very troubling. It was a long way around the coast of Australia, and the distance ate fuel and supplies. The torpedo problems bothered the captains, and at this point the submariners were not too sure of the Japanese routes of supply, so locating ships and ship lanes was a problem.

Admiral Lockwood's coming in the last days of May 1942 meant a big difference to the Southwest Pacific Command, because it gave the command more stature to have an admiral in charge. Even so the successes were rare because at this point the ships were not there. Japan was having difficulty resupplying her far-flung empire.

The S-boats, in spite of their small size and range, helped greatly to harry the Japanese in the Bismarck Archipelago, the Solomon Islands, and New Guinea.

Lieutenant Commander O. G. Kirk was the skipper of the *S-42*, an old boat that leaked oil when she dived, and could dive only about half as fast as a new fleet boat. In April he was assigned to go up to the Bismarck Archipelago and go hunting. Nothing much happened until May 11 when Kirk spotted the Japanese command ship *Okinoshima,* the flagship of the Japanese force that occupied Tulagi long before the battle of the Coral Sea. Kirk fired four torpedoes and got three hits which caused great fires, and eventually ended in the sinking of the ship. But then the counteraction came. The Japanese had several destroyers in the area and the call came to find and sink that submarine. The *S-42* was driven down deep and battered by depth charges. She was down for many hours. Since she had no air-conditioning, the strain on the crew was enormous. Several men collapsed. One man went temporarily insane, but somehow the sub managed to survive the depth-charging, and returned to Brisbane.

The *S-47* came in these same waters, where an American submarine could expect plenty of trouble. For not far away was the major southern naval base at Truk, sometimes called the Gibraltar of the Pacific. There were always many destroyers in these waters, plus patrol boats and patrol aircraft. The reward and the lure was the presence here of many big warships.

The *S-47* captain, Lieutenant Commander James W. Davis, spotted a cruiser but his little boat would not move fast enough so that he could get a shot at her, and he was detected by the cruisers' destroyer escort, which came after the S-boat with depth charges. This adventure was scarcely over when the *S-47* attacked a medium-sized freighter at periscope depth. The freighter turned and very nearly rammed the submarine. Then she got away.

The South Pacific was always dangerous water; nearly every islet was surrounded by a coral reef and much of the water was too dangerous for navigation. The charts, when there were any, were usually antiquated, made by some coastal copra traders around the turn of the century. That's why one summer night the *S-39* grounded on a reef off Rossel Island in the Louisiades, the scene of part of the action in the battle of the Coral Sea.

The boat stuck fast. The captain, Lieutenant F. E. Brown, tried to reverse engines, tried to blow ballast, tried to have the men move back and forth to rock the boat, but nothing helped. She was stuck fast, and in immediate danger of being spotted by the Japanese and attacked. For this was Japanese convoy country, very close to the enemy air bases. They even threw overboard the precious torpedoes and ammunition for the deck guns. But nothing helped, and it became apparent the boat would not be gotten off the reef. As the tide dropped, the boat's list became more pronounced until it reached 60 degrees. Lieutenant Brown used his radio, and finally got help in the form of the Australian corvette *Kratoomow*, which took all the men off after they had destroyed the codebooks and secret equipment. The submarine was then made the target for Allied bombers, and was destroyed by bombs.

By midsummer, the forces were in place, although the submarines were not making any spectacular successes. But one reason for this is that the battles of the Coral Sea and Midway had seriously disrupted the Japanese timetable for conquest. By this time, according to earlier calculations, the whole of New Guinea should have been in Japanese hands, and the occupation of Fiji, French Polynesia, and Samoa should have been under way. Australia should have been isolated, and under attack. But it had not happened, and the Japanese were having their difficulties in regrouping, and in securing adequate shipping from Japan to supply troops and military installations.

As Admiral Yamamoto sensed, the Japanese drive to conquest had peaked without achieving the final success of defeating the South Pacific Fleet, and the war was making a turnaround. It was not readily apparent in Tokyo, when a count of the ships of the Combined Fleet would prove Japan's superiority to the Americans.

With that sort of statistics in hand, the expansionists urged onward, not listening to the wiser heads who suggested that Japan should stop, regroup, and prepare to defend this new empire with no further ambitions to extending it.

CHAPTER EIGHTEEN

China, the Attrition War

By the summer of 1942 the Japanese army was deeply mired in the bog of China, its supply lines dangerously extended. The Japanese held the cities and the mail lines and the roads in the daytime. But at night the country was Chinese, and the Japanese troops in anything less than column strength were at risk every time they stepped out of a town.

General Matsui in 1938 announced the aims of the Japanese expeditionary force to be to protect Japanese property and lives, and "to establish the foundation of lasting peace in Eastern Asia." By 1942 they had done anything but that; in Tokyo they still called it the China incident, but it was a full-fledged war fought on a front almost 2,000 miles long.

In the winter of 1938–39 the Japanese government had finally despaired of dealing with the obdurate Chiang Kai-shek, who would not give up, and established their own puppet government at Nanking under Wang Ching-wei, a respected member of the Kuomintang party in years past. In 1940 he moved to Nanking and took over.

By the spring of 1941 the Nationalist government had moved to Chungking, far out west on the Yangtze River, and the Japanese were bombing the capital repeatedly, particularly after the war extended to the Pacific. By the time of the battle of the Coral Sea, Japan had seized Burma. Following the Doolittle raid on Tokyo, the infuriated Japanese had launched a campaign in eastern China to capture all the airfields that were used by the American Fourteenth Air Force, and initiated a fright campaign against the Chinese in which an estimated

500,000 people were killed for having helped the Doolittle fliers in some way.

But the Chinese never faltered; they retreated and harried the Japanese at night, and in the countryside. Although the Japanese held the coastal cities, American naval officers were landed on the coast and set up radio stations giving weather information and occasional news about convoys to the submarine commands in Australia and at Pearl Harbor.

The Americans attacked the major Japanese base at Hankow with bombers on July 1, seriously damaging the docks and warehouse facilities. And the war went on.

CHAPTER NINETEEN

The Aleutian Seas

The Aleutian Seas—one navy historian called them the world's worst. Certainly they rivaled the Baltic in chill and ferocity, cold and misery to the men who sailed the seas. And of all the ships that coursed these waters, the most affected were the submarines, the American S-boats which were uncomfortable enough by themselves, to say nothing of the times when they were coated with ice, and the interiors were down to subzero temperatures, or steaming from the cold.

Two of the boats, the *S-34* and the *S-35*, sailed out from Dutch Harbor on April 12, 1942. They were heading for the Japanese Kurile Islands and the game they might find. They had scarcely left port when they became separated.

On the second day out, Lieutenant Commander Thomas Wogan's *S-34* was damaged by a huge wave that washed over the bridge and nearly killed the quartermaster on duty. The boat made a great circle through the Bering Sea, and on April 22 was in Japanese waters, attacking a Japanese trawler. But the torpedo missed its target. Skipper Wogan took his boat through the Kuriles into the Sea of Okhotsk and came across a Japanese merchant ship, but its two torpedoes missed.

That was the end of the action with the enemy, but not the end of the voyage by far. The *S-34* ran into ice on her way back. The fog made it impossible to see on the surface. On May 1 the submarine anchored in Chichagof Harbor on Attu. They had one day of sunshine and fresh air; the next day turned foul, and soon they were fighting a storm. They got back to Dutch Harbor on May 10 with a score of zero.

Most of the patrols were like this, before the Japanese landed on Kiska and Attu Islands. The sea was so rugged that boats could not stand it long and crews had to be relieved after each patrol to go down south and take it easy a little, so that they could come back up and brave the arctic seas once more.

The Japanese occupied Kiska and Attu early in June, as noted. Two weeks later, Admiral Theobald, the American commander in the Aleutians, ordered Lieutenant H. L. Jukes to take the reconnaissance trip to Amchitka Island in the *S-27*. The submarine arrived at Amchitka and came to the surface to recharge her batteries. But fog swept into the area, and although she was five miles offshore, soon she found herself on a reef off Amchitka. The boat began to list, the motor flooded, and the batteries began to get wet and to slop over with fumes of chlorine gas, one of the deadly dangers of the submariner. The submarine sent a distress call, which was picked up, but the report of position was garbled. All hands then abandoned ship in a rubber boat, with food and supplies. Amchitka was deserted, but they found an abandoned church for shelter, and lived in the community left long ago by others, until rescued a week later by PBY flying boats.

The submarine was lost.

By this time, Admiral Nimitz had sent seven big fleet submarines to the Aleutians. This was more like it; these boats could operate well if not comfortably in the cold northern waters. Lieutenant Howard Gilmore took the *Growler* out on June 20 from Pearl Harbor, and went on station at Kiska.

For three days she dodged enemy planes, but on July 5 saw three destroyers off the entrance to Kiska Harbor. She approached and Skipper Gilmore fired four torpedoes, one at each destroyer and an extra one at the *Arare*. The destroyer fired back, but missed. The *Growler*'s torpedoes did not miss and did not malfunction for a change. The *Arare* was sunk, and the *Kasumi* and *Shiranuhi* were both damaged.

The problem, however, was that in the action, the *Growler*'s periscope had jammed, which made operations very difficult. Two days later she was still having problems, and that day she was spotted by a Japanese destroyer which came to make a depth-charge attack. The charges very nearly did hit the submarine, but she managed to escape with damaged propellers and sound gear. After darkness closed in, she surfaced and escaped and moved to Dutch Harbor where it was decided to send her back to Pearl Harbor for repairs. Much to the crew's delight she did not return to the frozen north.

The *Triton*, which had been cruising in the South Pacific that spring, came to the Aleutians in June, and took station off Azgattu Island, just off Attu on the fourth of July.

In the afternoon along came a destroyer, the *Nenohi*, steaming slowly through the northern mist. Skipper Kirkpatrick fired two torpedoes and took the boat down fast. A minute later he heard the explosion of one torpedo, and coming to periscope depth saw the *Nenohi* capsize. A hundred men clung to her bottom in the icy water. The fog soon lifted and the *Triton* moved out. She stayed in the area until July 12, when the periscope began to act up in the cold, and the ship went to Dutch Harbor for repairs. That took three days, and then the *Triton* went to Kiska, to join a bombardment group that was descending on the island. The cruisers did their work, there were no ships fleeing out of the harbor, as the *Triton* crew had hoped.

August was a month of the sort of patrol that the Aleutians sailors detested but had come to expect. A month of nothingness, mostly at sea, seeing nothing. The submarine did find one target and damaged the ship but did not sink it. She also was employed to carry an army reconnaissance unit from Dutch Harbor to Adak, a dangerous mission because it meant coming into shore, and one never knew what would happen with the Aleutian weather. In September the ordeal was ended, and she was sent back to the sunny Hawaiian Islands for a refit and a week at the Royal Hawaiian Hotel for the crew.

Admiral Nimitz, an old pigboat man himself from the days of the Philippine insurrection, knew what submariners wanted and needed. Rest and recreation, and he provided it in grand style, in the best hotel in the Hawaiian Islands of that day. That was what pigboat men wanted when a patrol was over—rest, first-class surroundings, clean sheets, plenty of drinks, good food, and girls. All these were provided to the best of the command's ability, and the submarine force lived a luxurious life—when they were not putting their necks on the line for months at a time. They were much envied, but no one could really fault them; theirs was the most dangerous game, and if a boat went down, that was the end for 80 or more men. It was a precarious, frightening, and exciting existence, and it took a man with a certain sense of fatalism and enormous courage to stand the gaff.

The Aleutians watch continued, gray and grim. Lieutenant Commander T. C. Abele brought the *Grunion* up to Kiska in July. She had some excitement; in two weeks in mid-July she attacked five Japanese subchasers, sank two, and damaged a third one. But there were five of them. On July 30 the *Grunion* signaled that the enemy had undertaken very strong antisubmarine warfare around Kiska, employing destroyers as well as subchasers. And then the *Grunion* was silent. They never heard from her again at Dutch Harbor or at Pearl. She had fallen victim to the enemy.

The dispatch of the big fleet submarines to the Aleutians had been an experiment, and in the late summer of 1942 Admiral Nimitz had to acknowledge that it was not a very successful one. Not that the fleet boats did not comport themselves well, they did, but the force investment, and the number of ships they could sink in Japan's home and southern waters was so much greater, that it was a shame to waste them on the northern station.

By October 1942 the fleet boat usage was winding down. Army and navy staff men had a bright idea: use aircraft to find targets for the fleet boats. This was tried with the *Halibut*, but communications were not good enough, and to be frank, aviators were not always very good at pinpointing positions. On October 21, the real problem became apparent. The *Halibut* was in position to see a PBY attacking a Japanese ship, but the fog was so thick she could not see the ship. The *Halibut* came up, and made a surface approach and fired torpedoes at this luscious target. But something happened. At least one of the torpedoes passed under the ship without exploding (they were using the magnetic exploder) and then the Japanese ships returned the compliment and fired a torpedo and laid several shots from a deck gun that had earlier been concealed. She was, said the *Halibut*, a Q-ship. Japanese records do not show the use of Q-ships in the Aleutians, but that does not mean it was not done, because the records in Tokyo did not always conform to those at the Japanese outfitting stations, and most of them were lost during the last stages of the war.

By some alert maneuvering the men of the *Halibut* got out of trouble in a hurry and got out of that area, too.

So in the Aleutians in the fall of 1942 it was back to the S-boats. One reason for this was the paucity of targets, and that was caused by the changed plans of the Japanese in the autumn of 1942. They realized that their chances of making use of the Attu and Kiska stations were remote, and they could not expend the resources to make resupply a regular matter. So the garrisons on Attu and Kiska languished in the cold and miserable weather, and the Japanese turned their attention elsewhere, as did the Americans.

The S-boats, which were really very hard to employ in the new sort of warfare due to their limited range, were still valuable up here in the north. On October 26, the *S-31* sighted a 3,000-ton merchant ship. Lieutenant Commander Robert F. Sellars was patrolling on the normal Japanese supply route which led from the Japanese Kurile Islands to the American Aleutians. She was in enemy territory in Paramushiro when she found the ship, and saw that it was anchored in the open road. What an opportunity; the skipper fired two shots, and sank her. But when the boat went down, suddenly it hit bottom much sooner than anyone had expected, and then came the fear of retaliatory blows. But none came, and still it was a perilous passage, because they had to make their way out at periscope depth trying to find a course through the reefs to deep water, having available only the sort of charts the American mariners had of Japanese waters in those days—highly inaccurate.

The *S-31* traveled 14,000 miles on this patrol for one sinking. It was not the most advantageous way to fight the enemy, but still the Aleutians patrol had to be maintained as long as the Japanese had a presence in the American world.

It was dangerous, uncomfortable, unpleasant, as negative an experience as was suffered by any unit of World War II; it made courage an everyday matter, and rewarded it with very little.

Here is how American navy historian Samuel Eliot Morison described the experience of the *S-35* on a December 1942 patrol in the Aleutians.

An arctic blow came up on 21 December and the submarine crawled desperately up and down the steep slopes of pale green frigid waves which frequently inundated the tiny bridge. On the second dogwatch, a savage wave slammed Lieutenant Henry S. Monroe into a hatch, spraining an arm and a leg. He limped painfully below, and turned in only to be routed out by the dread shout of fire from the control room where salt water had short-circuited electric cables. Crackling white electric arcs and wicked blue flames lit up the control room, when one fire was quenched another broke out. Noxious fumes forced the men to secure the engines and drove them topside. The sailors worked desperately, as they were in imminent danger of grounding on Amchitka but finally they put out the fires, and restarted the engines. Next morning fire broke out again, and since there were no flame-extinguishing chemicals left, all hands were driven to the exposed bridge where they huddled miserably, praying that the fire would suffocate for want of air. All day the struggle continued, engineers alternating between smoky interior and icy topside. Eventually Monroe and his men won.

CHAPTER TWENTY

Planning the Offensive

Plan Orange, the United States Navy war plan for the Pacific war, had been drawn years before 1941; it envisaged a Japanese attack, an American withdrawal from the Western Pacific, and then an offensive across the Central Pacific to win the war. In other words, from the outset, the American navy bosses had known that they could not hold the Western Pacific initially.

When Plan Orange was drawn there was no war in Europe or any commitment by the United States, but after mid-December 1942, when British Prime Minister Winston Churchill came to America, President Roosevelt then pledged U.S. commitment to fight the Germans first, and then take on the Japanese.

This indicated a holding action and no more in the Pacific. The Pacific theater could not expect more than a minimum of planes and ships and armaments. The big thrust had to go to Europe, and early in 1942 the army and the War Production Administration were putting their efforts into the plans for a second front. At first the plans were too ambitious, but they were refined to become the North African invasion.

But Admiral King's eye was always on the Pacific, and in February 1942 he began laying the groundwork for a Pacific offensive. He advised General George C. Marshall, the chief of staff of the U.S. Army, that he wanted to establish an American base on Efate, an island 25 miles long and 14 miles wide in the New Hebrides, 600 miles southeast of Guadalcanal. This base would strengthen the Allied position in Australia, which was obviously under threat by the Japanese. Further, it would be the first base of several needed for a drive through the Solomon Islands, to destroy the Japanese base at Rabaul and then the big naval base at Truk.

Admiral King reiterated this argument to President Roosevelt in March 1942, at a time when the Pacific war situation was at its most desperate. The Japanese had advanced everywhere with uncanny ease. It was apparent that the Philippines could not be saved. The Allied defense of the Dutch East Indies was collapsing and some Americans were talking about abandoning Australia and New Zealand to whatever fate held for them. But Admiral King argued that Australia could not be abandoned, any more than could Britain, and President Roosevelt, who had a strong feeling for English-speaking unity, agreed with him. There above Australia the line must be drawn. A consolidation of defenses must be made there. The Japanese drive must be stopped. This was regarded as so important that the Joint Chiefs of Staff considered the possibility of reversing the decision to fight first in Europe.

The Joint Chiefs also decided that they would have to send at least 40,000 troops to the Pacific. About half that number were already there, or en route to the MacArthur command, which was just being moved to Australia in March 1942. So the Joint Chiefs agreed to attempt to contain the Japanese, while exerting maximum effort in the European theater.

So a garrison of 500 men from the American Division in New Caledonia was sent up to Efate along with Marine Fighter Squadron 212, and the Fourth Marine Defense Battalion.

The Southern Pacific area was divided into two major commands, one based in Australia under General MacArthur, and the other based at Pearl Harbor, under Admiral Nimitz. Vice Admiral Robert Ghormley, recently the naval attaché in London, was chosen to be subcommander under Nimitz of the South Pacific Force, with his headquarters at Auckland, New Zealand.

Ghormley assembled a staff in Washington and headed for the Pacific. He stopped off at Pearl Harbor and picked up Rear Admiral John S. McCain, who would be his chief of land-based aircraft in the island command. McCain then went to Nouméa, which would be his headquarters.

The movement in the South Pacific was continual. While Admiral Ghormley was in Hawaii, the battle of the Coral Sea was fought, and the Japanese move against Port Moresby was forestalled. But the Japanese had installed a seaplane base at Tulagi, even though the Allies had destroyed their first batch of planes.

The Americans then built a base at Espiritu Santo, which would become very important.

Late in May, although Admiral Nimitz was preoccupied with the Midway problem, he suggested that the First Marine Raider Battalion be used to make a raid on Tulagi. But General MacArthur was not interested in Tulagi or the Solomon Islands. The Japanese had established bases at Lae and Salamaua in British New Guinea, and he could see that they still intended to try to capture Port Moresby. His preoccupation was with the New Guinea situation so he rejected that idea. Thus the Americans lost a chance to occupy the Guadalcanal area when the Japanese backs were turned and their major naval units were heading for Midway. No one in the Allied camp knew it, but the Japanese had already issued plans for the occupation of New Caledonia, Fiji, and Samoa, and these moves would have been carried out had not the Japanese fleet been badly battered at Midway.

The center of Japanese activity then became Rabaul. A new Eighth Fleet was created under Vice Admiral Gunichi Mikawa and he arrived at Rabaul in June with five heavy cruisers, three light cruisers, and a dozen destroyers. The Japanese began building up the Twenty-fifth Air Flotilla at Rabaul so they had 245 bombers and 300 fighters at Rabaul, plus several seaplanes and 10 seaplane fighters, and a modified Zero at Tulagi. They were building four more air bases on New Britain, New Ireland, at Lae and Salamaua, and on Buka, a small island at the north end of Bougainville. The Americans did not know it but Admiral Yamamoto was also planning another air base on Guadalcanal, and, as soon as Port Moresby would be captured, to put a base there. Then the Japanese would be set for a drive against Australia.

Back at Pearl Harbor, Admiral Nimitz had been reinforced for the first time, and now had four carrier task forces at his disposal. After Midway Admiral Spruance had come ashore at Pearl Harbor to be chief of staff to Nimitz, and Admiral Fletcher had taken over the carrier *Enterprise*.

Captain Marc Mitscher of the *Hornet* had been promoted to Rear Admiral and was now commander of the *Hornet* task force. Rear Admiral Aubrey Fitch, who had commanded the old *Lexington* when she was sunk at the battle of the Coral Sea, had been given command of the *Saratoga* task force, and Rear Admiral Leigh Noyes had been given command of the *Wasp* task force. Not only had the Japanese suffered at Midway, but the American carrier air groups had lost many pilots. Torpedo Eight had been completely decimated, and the torpedo squadrons of the other Midway carriers were badly hit. Fighter and dive-bomber squadrons had also suffered losses. This brought to the attention of Admiral Nimitz the need for a better and faster carrier pilot training program, and he brought the matter to the attention of Admiral King and the Washington high command. Thus the American naval air training program was improved, and the Americans began to overcome the Japanese air force superiority both in numbers and in skilled pilots, for the Japanese had no plans to change their ways.

In June Admirals Fletcher and Mitscher were warned that they were on 48-hour notice at Pearl Harbor, which meant they were in a training program. Fitch was busy ferrying aircraft to Midway Island to replace the planes lost there in the battle, and the *Wasp* had just come through the Panama Canal from service in the Mediterranean.

What were the Americans to do now?

General MacArthur had a plan. Give him the troops and the ships and he would assault and capture Rabaul, the Japanese base.

Could it be done?

MacArthur said yes. The navy said no, not with the forces the navy had. There were not enough warships, or enough planes, or enough supply ships to do the job. The Japanese navy, despite the loss of those four carriers, still had more carriers than the American navy and was still the most powerful navy afloat. Until there could be a big buildup of forces, the navy did not want to go up against Rabaul, the center of Japanese power in the Southern Pacific.

The fact was that at the moment the United States was not in a position to undertake a major assault in the Pacific except in some more or less isolated place. Tulagi appealed to the navy, because it would give them a foothold in the Solomons, preparatory to a great advance later. In a memo to General Marshall, MacArthur suggested the use of the First Marine Division somewhere in the Southern Pacific. Nimitz liked the idea too and was ready to use two of his carrier task forces to support such a move. General Marshall also liked the idea, but as a loyal army man, he suggested that it had to be a navy show because the marines were navy troops and the navy would support the action. All MacArthur could do was support with land-based air.

Nimitz flew to San Francisco for a meeting with Admiral King. On July 2 the Joint Chiefs of Staff issued a directive calling for the ultimate occupation of the New Britain–Rabaul–New Ireland–New Guinea area, with a target date of August 1. Three days later, Admiral Nimitz had word that an American reconnaissance plane had flown over Guadalcanal Island and observed that the Japanese were starting to build an airfield there. Meanwhile in the Southwest Pacific, General MacArthur was very unhappy when he learned that the Joint Chiefs had proposed that the next military operation be put in the hands of the navy. Admiral Ghormley came up from New Zealand to Melbourne to confer with MacArthur, his chief of staff General Sutherland, and Vice Admiral Arthur S. Carpender, who had just been appointed chief of the Southwest Pacific Naval Forces—in other words to be commander of MacArthur's navy. They did not like anything about the operation, probably for different reasons. But they could agree that they did not want anything done around August 1. It was too soon for them. The Allies did not have enough planes, or enough airfields, and the whole operation would be likely to run into disaster.

They so told King and Nimitz on July 8th. King observed to General Marshall that this was quite a turnaround for MacArthur, who just three weeks before had said he was prepared to capture Rabaul if they would give him a couple of carriers and a division of marines. So it was obvious that MacArthur's ego was hurting and King paid no attention to that.

King wrote MacArthur that the situation was very serious, and they must not let the Japanese have an airfield that could stop the forthcoming movement which he expected then to be into the Santa Cruz Islands as well as Tulagi. They had to stop the Japanese and stop them right there. King knew very well that he was undertaking an operation of great importance without adequate backup resources, but he felt the absolute necessity to do so in order to protect the lifeline to Australia. And of course he was right, as the Japanese plans for the area show. After the war, these plans would be made public. Had the Japanese been allowed to move their next steps would have been into the islands around Australia, and then to Australia.

CHAPTER TWENTY-ONE

Operation Shoestring

From the beginning Admiral Ghormley did not like the Guadalcanal invasion. He and General MacArthur referred to it as Operation Shoestring, and they were not alone. There was the First Marine Division and attached troops, and that was the force. There were no reserves except back in French Oceania where the American Division of 22,000 men was headquartered. But all those troops were needed where they were and there was no manpower to spare.

Even so Admiral Ghormley had to admit that he had enough ships and men to do the job, just barely. The big unknown factor was the power of the Japanese land-based air force, centered around Rabaul—from which the ships of the American force would have to be protected. The responsibility for this in the initial phase before the airfield could be secured and used would have to lie with the American carrier fleet. That was expected.

To assist, Admiral Nimitz sent a thousand men of the army air force ground crews down to Admiral Ghormley and announced the buildup of the B-17 bomber force to 35 planes. The big problem, as everyone could see, was going to be manpower.

In June Admiral King told Rear Admiral Richmond Kelly Turner that he had a new assignment for him.

A sea command? asked Turner, who for months had been pestering King for the opportunity to go to sea.

Well, yes and no, said Admiral King. It was something new. The U.S. Navy was about to embark on the reconquest of the

Japanese empire, and Turner was the man who was going to manage the amphibious landings as they moved across the Pacific.

So Admiral Turner began his planning and arrived in Wellington on July 18 to take command.

One division was in training. One regiment, the Seventh Marines, had gone to Samoa in March. The First and Fifth Regiments were expecting to have six months of training in New Zealand. Elements of the division were loaded aboard two transports, the *Wakefield* and the *Ericsson*. The ships sailed from California. Major General Alexander A. Vandegrift, the division commander, was with them. They arrived at Wellington and Vandegrift thought he was going into a training program. It was almost two weeks later, June 26, when he learned that the division was going into combat within six weeks.

For the next few weeks the marines trained in a camp about 35 miles from Wellington, but not for six months, only from June 15 to July 1. Then it was back to Wellington to lead four transports with their gear and weapons and supplies.

The division was split in three elements, part of it sailing from Samoa, part from California, and part from New Zealand. The rendezvous for the invasion force would be Fiji.

General Vandegrift was appalled at the charts and maps given him. They were turn-of-the-century materials, and there was nothing newer. So he sent a team of intelligence personnel to Australia to interview former planters and others who knew the Solomons. They did not get much useful military information. Military personnel had not had any reason to visit Guadalcanal in peacetime, and the sort of information that travelers had was not of much use.

The most useful information came from aerial photographs and a reconnaissance flight made by two marine officers in a B-17. They checked on the terrain at Tulagi, but they were chased away by Japanese float planes from the seaplane base before they could get a good look at the Guadalcanal side.

If all this had occurred two or three months earlier, the marines would have had the benefit of some more intelligence via the radio interception of Japanese messages. But just before the Midway operation, the Japanese changed their naval codes, and the radio intelligence teams had a great deal of difficulty with messages for several months thereafter. They got through Midway, but then there came a blank, just as the Guadalcanal operation was in progress.

By July 16 the pessimists in the fleet were sure that the target date of August 1 was impossible to achieve, and so Admiral Ghormley postponed the operation for six days.

But while that was not much time, it was in another sense a great deal of time, because air observation showed that the airfield on Guadalcanal was nearly ready for use, and Admiral King knew that Admiral Yamamoto would lose no time in using it to stage bombers down from Rabaul to attack the cities and military installations of Australia.

Everyone concerned, one would expect, would be enthusiastic about this chance to hit the enemy. But that was not the case. Admiral Ghormley's enthusiasm was very slight, and Admiral Fletcher questioned the wisdom of the whole operation. This was most unfortunate, the two top tactical commanders being out of step with the high command; in fact, Admiral Fletcher's reluctance was such that he very nearly wrecked the invasion in the beginning.

Fletcher was to be in tactical command of the invasion. Admiral Turner was to deliver the troops to shore, and then General Vandegrift was to take command of the fighting on land. These two splendid officers did their jobs to perfection, and were responsible for saving the invasion when it occurred. To be sure, the questioners had a good point: the Americans were not ready to launch a major military strike at this point; but had they not done so at precisely this time, the outcome of the Pacific war might have been quite different. Ultimately, the Allies would have triumphed but in all probability not before most of the cities of Australia—at least in the north— had been seriously damaged by Japanese bombing, and the Japanese probably would have been so foolish as to undertake an invasion of Australia. The impetus to empire was very strong in 1942; the Japanese had already overextended themselves, but they were caught in a vise of their own making. Having embarked on the program of conquest, the leaders felt they must complete it to protect what they had won, and to some that meant taking control of Australia and New Zealand to finish the Pacific sweep.

CHAPTER TWENTY-TWO

Guadalcanal Landing

The war was rushing everyone and everything along. The landings were scheduled for Guadalcanal on August 1 and then rescheduled for August 7, but by July 15, no one really knew what was going to happen, because Admiral Ghormley was just issuing his operational plan.

But Admiral Turner, the man who would do the job, knew what he was going to do. He had 19 transports and cargo ships and four old four-stack destroyers converted for transport work since they were no longer first-class fighting ships. He had four cruisers and six destroyers for protection against the Japanese. He had five more old destroyers, now converted to be minesweepers, to clear the channels and the roadsteads. Rear Admiral V. A. C. Crutchley of the Royal Australian Navy was to command a group of four cruisers and nine destroyers, one cruiser and all nine destroyers being American. Vice Admiral Fletcher was to bring two carriers and the supporting ships to keep the Japanese aircraft away. Further air protection would be given and reconnaissance made by Ádmiral McCain's shore-based aircraft. By the end of July new airfields had been built, the seaplane tender *Curtiss* had moved to Espirtu Santo, and B-17s were keeping the Solomon Islands under observation. The landings would be made on Guadalcanal, under General Vandegrift, and on Tulagi across the sound by Brigadier General W. H. Rupertus.

The ships involved would be coming from California, Nouméa, Sydney, and Wellington. They would meet 400 miles southeast of the Fiji Islands.

165

On the morning of July 26 Admirals Turner, Kinkaid, Noyes, McCain, and Callaghan and General Vandegrift met aboard Admiral Fletcher's flagship, the *Saratoga,* off Fiji. Admiral Ghormley was not there. He should have been, for had he come, he might have recognized then and there the problem that Fletcher was about to create, and perhaps by some gentle pressure he could have stopped it.

At the conference Admiral Fletcher dropped a bombshell. He would support the landings of the marines, as ordered, but he would not support them for more than 48 hours.

When Admiral Turner heard this he erupted. For he knew precisely what he was going to face, and he could see his only air support backing out on him, for that is precisely what Fletcher was doing. He was afraid he would lose another carrier. He had come under considerable criticism for his handling of the *Yorktown,* which need never have been lost, and almost everybody at Pearl Harbor knew it. He was not going to put himself in danger of criticism again—he thought. The best way to solve the problem was to stay out of harm's way—he thought. Since Admiral Fletcher was senior officer present, his word was law, and there was nothing to be done about it. Admiral Turner and General Vandegrift agreed that they needed air support while their supplies were being unloaded at Guadalcanal. Fletcher turned a deaf ear. And that was that. There was no Nimitz to whom they could appeal here, and Ghormley was not where he should have been, aboard that flagship.

There was scarcely time for Admiral Turner to worry about this bad twist that fate had taken, for he had to get his amphibious rehearsal over with. This was held in the Fijis between July 28 and July 31. The landings were a bust. No one knew there was a coral reef between the ships and the shore of the island, and so they came up against it and only a handful of landing craft made their way through openings to shore. Hurry, hurry, hurry, and make mistakes. That's the way it was.

There was no time to try again. The next landing would be real and they had to expect the place to be bristling with the enemy. The ships formed up and away they went toward battle.

The goal was Cape Esperance, Guadalcanal Island. At 8 P.M. on August 6 the leading ships were 60 miles south of the Guadalcanal shore. As far as they knew their approach was completely secret. It had all been done so quickly there had been no excessive radio traffic, which usually was the giveaway about activity. The weather between Rabaul and the south had been bad, so the Japanese search planes had not spotted the little fleet.

Morning came and the ships entered the sound that lies between Tulagi and Guadalcanal.

Radio Tulagi, the Japanese station, then broadcast:

"A large force of ships of unknown number and kind is entering the sound. What can these ships be?"

So the surprise was complete.

The Japanese, so accustomed to easy victory, did not even know what was about to hit them. It was D-Day, and then came a message over the squawk box of every ship.

"Now hear this. Now hear this . . ."

A statement from Admiral Turner.

"On August 7 this force will recapture Tulagi and Guadalcanal Islands which are now in the hands of the enemy.

"In this first forward step toward clearing the Japanese out of conquered territory we have strong support from the Pacific Fleet and from the air, surface, and submarine forces in the South Pacific and Australia.

"It is significant of victory that we see here shoulder to shoulder the United States Navy, Marines, and Army and the Australian and New Zealand air, naval, and army services.

"I have confidence that all elements of this armada will in skill and courage show themselves fit comrades of those brave men who have already dealt the enemy mighty blows for a great cause.

"God bless you all."

Then the squawk boxes went dead, and the men contemplated the great adventure that was to begin in a matter of hours. It was 3 A.M. and the transports bound for Tulagi separated from those bound for Guadalcanal. It was a silent night and a silent morning.

There was no sign of life on either Florida Island, where Tulagi was located, or the big island of Guadalcanal, although the Japanese were there. The Americans expected to encounter at least 5,000 enemy troops on Guadalcanal. About Tulagi they were much less clear; they knew the seaplane base was there, but they did not know how much else the Japanese had brought in.

Just after six o'clock in the morning, the cruiser *Quincy* began the bombardment of Lunga Point on the west coast of Guadalcanal. Overhead the fighters of the combat air patrol looked down, and one of the pilots spotted a small schooner, moving between Tulagi and Guadalcanal. The fighter went down to the deck and machine-gunned the schooner; it was carrying gasoline, which burned, and the schooner sank.

The other warships assigned to bombardment also began firing. Forty-four fighters and bombers from the carriers *Enterprise* and *Saratoga* attacked other shore installations as scheduled.

At 6:45 the transports moved in toward the beach at Guadalcanal, in the area between Koli Point and the Tenaru River just east of the Tenaru. Five minutes later the landing began with the rising sun. The boats came in, and the men were ready for action. They were riding in Higgins landing boats, and some other landing craft capable of carrying a tank. They started about three miles from shore, and the journey was a long slow one. It was just after 9 A.M. that the first troops reached the beach.

The minesweepers looked for mines, but found none, and so the ships moved in closer to the shore. The troops ashore, expecting trouble, found none. Only later did they learn why: most of the troops on Guadalcanal were construction workers, and altogether there were only 2,200 Japanese on the island. The Americans landed in division strength, and the sight was overwhelming. The Japanese were concentrated in the Kukum area, and they fled into the hills. The troops approached one mess hall, and found the food still warm on the table, but no Japanese.

All day long the troops landed and brought in equipment

and supplies. By afternoon the supplies were stacked up on the beach because no provision had been made for working parties to move the supplies away. The marines had expected a fight, but now by evening they had 11,000 men on Guadalcanal and no fight had developed.

The logistic problem was serious; landing craft circled outside the beach, waiting for a place to come in and drop their supplies. Men worked far into the night, but had to stop even though they had plenty of artifical light, because of congestion on the beach. All this was the more serious because of Fletcher's deadline. He was giving them only 48 hours before he withdrew and left the marines unprotected from air attack. Nearly half of that time was gone.

The first combat team began to organize the beach since there was no fighting to be done, but got hung up for most of the day. The second combat team marched west along the beach, and a third team pushed southwest through the jungle into the mountainous interior, hoping to capture Mount Austen. But the maps they had were hopelessly inaccurate and Mount Austen proved to be much farther away than it had appeared. The mountain was actually nine miles from the mouth of the Tenaru River. Both combat teams moved forward early on August 8, encountering only a handful of Japanese. They learned that most of the Japanese had gone to Kukum near Lunga Point, where the main buildings were located.

When General Vandegrift learned how far Mount Austen was, he abandoned that part of the plan and told Colonel Hunt to take his team to capture Kukum and the mouth of the Lunga River. At noon, when the marines crossed the Lunga, they encountered rifle fire and machine gun fire. They eliminated this problem and then moved into a littered Japanese camp at about 3 P.M.

Meanwhile Colonel C. B. Cates and his men headed toward the airfield. By late afternoon they reached it and occupied the area. There were no planes, but the airfield was ready to receive them.

At the end of the day, the Japanese had been scattered. The marines held Guadalcanal, with an airfield. The Japanese had also brought down machine tools and established machine shops for the use of the airfield personnel. They had electric lights, an air-compressor plant to service aerial torpedoes, and a great store of dried and canned food. Casualties had been minimal, and the Guadalcanal operation seemed to be a walk-in. The last part of the day was spent consolidating camps and trying to clear up the beach where all the supplies had been stacked up. In fact, the landing place was moved to another beach west of the Tenaru River. But General Vandegrift and Admiral Turner were under no illusions. They knew about all that land-based air strength of the enemy at Rabaul, and they knew it would be used when the Japanese overcame their surprise.

The marines had learned from the enemy prisoners that this was really just a work battalion and that no military action had been expected. That was certain to change, too.

On the morning of August 7 the second group of transports headed across the sound toward Tulagi, the site of the Japanese seaplane base that had already been attacked once by the American carrier planes, during the battle of the Coral Sea.

The seaplane base was on the little island of Tulagi. Only two miles long, it lay in the shadow of big Florida Island, which was 18 miles across the sound from the beaches of Guadalcanal. The island had been the capital of the Solomon Islands protectorate held by Australia. It comprised a cluster of Chinese shops and native huts and a residence house, a few other houses, a cricket field, courthouse, and a golf links. The colonial rulers did themselves well, and the Japanese had captured it all intact.

Across from Tulagi lies the island of Gavutu, from which a causeway ran to Tanambogo Island. The Lever Brothers Company of America had built offices and other installations here in the prewar years for the copra trade. It was here that the Japanese had built the seaplane base, in protected water. This place, unlike Guadalcanal, was dug in, ready for battle. There were more than 1,500 troops on the three islands; how many more is still unknown. Long after the battle, bulldozers uncovered bodies that had never been counted, in caves and dugouts. Japanese records were, of course, lost.

Admiral Turner and General Vandegrift and General Rupertus, the Tulagi commander of marines, had worked out a plan to land on the northern unsettled part of Tulagi, on what they called Beach Blue. They expected a stout enemy defense of the southern part of the island.

To attack Gavutu the marines would have to come into the harbor. Therefore marine units were landed early at Helvo and Haleta to forestall the enemy's setting up guns to fire on the approaching boats.

The landing on Beach Blue was made at 8 A.M. by the men of Lieutenant Colonel Merritt A. Edson's First Raider Battalion, who waded ashore on the beach. The Japanese had spotted the earlier landings at Halevo and Haleta, and had radioed Rabaul that the enemy was coming in.

The Raiders moved across into the jungle and crossed the ridge of the island to the settlement of Sesape and then down along the eastern shore. A second wave advanced along the ridge and the western shore. Behind them came a team of the Fifth Marines.

Radio Tulagi broadcast a little longer, warning Rabaul of the attack by highly superior strength. Then Radio Tulagi was overwhelmed by a salvo of high-explosive shells from the cruiser *San Juan*. That was the end of Radio Tulagi, and the last the Japanese knew of the invasion for a number of hours.

Unfortunately the naval bombardment was not very effective. In his history of the campaign, Samuel Elliot Morison indicates that its lack of effectiveness was due to the Allies inexperience; but more probably it was because of Japanese experience and skill in digging in. Throughout the war, many bombardments were carried out and as the marines General Holland Smith would complain, they never seemed to be enough. But the fault, if there was one, did not really lie with inexperience. Three ships fired 1,500 rounds of shell into the height called Hill 208 where the Japanese dug in, but the shells did not kill or flush out the enemy. Dive-bombers from the aircraft carriers struck the positions on the east, but the Japanese stood fast. They also used techniques learned in the China war that served very well in southern climes. Snipers roped themselves into palm trees, concealed by fronds. The snipers tied down troops for a while. The marines asked for more fire support, but something happened to the message and no support came. This sniper technique would be refined and the Japanese on New Guinea would set up a defense in depth in which they let the enemy pass them, and then shot them in the back.

Lieutenant Colonel Edson was ashore before 11:30 and he called a conference of his company commanders to assess the situation. Several high points were giving trouble. He led them to attack southeast, toward Hill 230 at the end of the island. The Japanese were dug in here and in the cricket field.

As darkness settled down on August 7 the Japanese had been ejected from most areas, but they still held Hill 281 and from this point they made several counterattacks in the middle of the night. By this time the battalion had set up its command post in the old colonial residency and one Japanese attack got through to the command post. But it did not succeed in routing the Americans, and although the enemy made noise all night, exhibiting a fright campaign that was well-planned, it did not work.

The marines of Tulagi had their troubles, but they were not as serious as those of the First Parachute Battalion, which was given the task of taking Gavutu and Tanambogo.

That assault began with aerial bombardment early in the morning. American carrier planes bombed and strafed the seaplane base, again destroying the new complement of planes, 19 float planes and two flying boats. Then the naval bombardment began, but once again the Japanese retreated to caves and holes and hid out and the bombardment was relatively ineffective.

It was about noon when the parachute battalion moved in. They had a rough trip by boat from their destroyer transport, about nine miles circling through the reef, then landed at the seaplane ramp. One destroyer came into harbor and shot up the defenders some more, but when the troops landed they were met by heavy fire. Major R. H. Williams, the battalion commander, was one of the casualties. As they landed, the machine guns opened up from the hills, and they were coming up against the coconut and earthen pillboxes that the Japanese built very well. The casualty rate for the parachute troops was one man in ten, and most were pinned down on the beach. But on the left flank they got a foothold, and overran Hill 148 on Gavutu and raised Old Glory before nightfall.

As night approached, the three islands were still full of Japanese who were still full of fight. During the afternoon the ships gave fire support on Tanambogo, and so did the bombers and fighters from the carriers. Most of the palm trees were stripped of foliage and felled before the day was out. But the firing of the causeway between Gavutu and Tanambogo was withering.

General Rupertus now found use for the troops who had landed at Haleta that morning, and sent half of them in boats to reinforce the marines on Gavutu and half to come around from the rear and attack Tanambogo. He ordered up a ship bombardment to help, and at dusk the ships began to fire. A shell from a destroyer exploded a gasoline tank in the darkness, and lit up the scene, just as the three boatloads of marines arrived at Tanambogo. The Japanese opened fire, and killed or wounded every man in one boat, and cut down most of the men in the other two boats. So the landing was a failure and the survivors went to Gavutu. Tanombogo and Tulagi were still held by the Japanese.

On the morning of August 8 two battalions of the Second Marine Regiment landed on Beach Blue to give a hand, and by mid-morning Hill 281 had been captured and Tulagi was virtually clear of Japanese—living Japanese. True to the tradition of the army's new *bushidō,* the Japanese nearly all fought to the death. Of perhaps a thousand Japanese soldiers on Tulagi, only three prisoners were taken, and some 50 Japanese escaped by swimming over to Florida Island and disappearing into the rugged hills.

"Each Jap fought until he was killed," General Vandegrift later said. "Each machine gun crew fought to the last man, who almost invariably killed himself rather than surrender.''

Life was very easy over on Guadalcanal where the service troops and construction troops had fled to the interior before the marine onslaught, so the transports *Adams* and *Hayes* were loaded with the Second and Third battalions of the Second Marine Regiment, which were then sent over to Tulagi. Lieutenant Colonel Hunt's battalion was sent to help out on Tanambogo.

The men landed on Gavutu just before noon on August 8 but immediately ran into the block of the causeway, which was swept by Japanese fire. Colonel Hunt loaded men and a tank into each of two LCMs and sent them around the reefs to the inside beach of Tanambogo. They went in mid-afternoon, covered by fire from the destroyer *Buchanan*.

The first tank landed safely but the tank crew was not very careful. They got out ahead of their supporting infantry, and the Japanese saw this and came rushing out of their defensive positions, stalled the tank with an iron bar thrust into the tread, and then hurled hand grenades into the apertures, killing all but one of the members of the crew.

The crew of the second tank was more cautious. They stuck with their infantrymen, about two-thirds of a company, and moved around Tanambogo, blasting dugouts that controlled the fire on the causeway. By ten o'clock on the night of August 8 the Japanese were reduced to a few snipers holed up in caves.

The Tulagi complex had been successfully assaulted, although it cost the marines 108 killed and 140 men wounded. The Japanese had lost between 1,500 and 2,000 men.

So Guadalcanal with little trouble and Tulagi with much trouble had been secured. But the enemy was really yet to be heard from, as General Vandegrift and Admiral Turner knew very well.

The last broadcast from Radio Tulagi had been made at 7:15 in the morning of August 7. In minutes at Rabaul, Admiral Yamada's Twenty-fifth Air Flotilla had been notified of the landings. At 9 A.M., the admiral gave orders to the Fifth and Sixth Air Attack Forces to head for Guadalcanal and Tulagi and at 10:45 an Australian coast-watcher on Bougainville sighted a large number of twin-engined bombers heading southeast. The word was passed to Admiral Turner at Guadalcanal.

At 1:15 that afternoon, the radar operator of the cruiser *Chicago* picked up the blips of many aircraft which were still 45 miles out. These were level bombers and they came in at high altitude, and did not hit anything. Two hours later came two groups of dive-bombers to attack the American ships off Guadalcanal. They scored a hit on the destroyer *Mugford* that killed about 20 men, but did not do too much damage to the ship.

The carriers *Enterprise* and *Saratoga* furnished protection against the Japanese. The first group of fighters was given the wrong coordinates for the Japanese, and so got lost and were out of the fight. Three other groups of eight fighters each tangled with the enemy, and claimed to have shot down several planes. One American group got into real trouble. Six Wildcat fighters went up against the bombers and their Zero escort, and five of the planes were shot down. Three pilots were lost but two were recovered. Sixteen fighters from the *Saratoga* went up to intercept the Japanese over Savo Island, but did not have time to gain altitude and were bounced by the enemy, who shot down five of the American planes. Another group of *Saratoga* fighters intercepted 11 Japanese dive-bombers and claimed to have shot down all of them. The *Wasp*'s fighters were running combat air patrol over the carrier formation so they did not get into the action. Several of her dive-bombers did, however; they attacked Tulagi and were attacked by the Japanese in turn. One dive-bomber was shot down.

So the Americans lost 11 fighters and one dive-bomber that day, but they saved the transports from the enemy attacks.

On August 8 the Japanese came back, this time with torpedo bombers. Just before noon, a group of twin-engined bombers and single-engined bombers bearing torpedoes came in low over Florida Island. Three fighters were on patrol over the ships, and they jumped four bombers and chased them off. The rest bored in on the ships but the antiaircraft barrage put up was fearsome, and 17 bombers were shot down. Nine got through the ship formation, and one connected. The plane was afire and the pilot steered it into the transport *George F. Elliott*, and set her afire. The crew panicked and abandoned ship, and there was no one to fight the fires but one destroyer and that was not enough. The *Elliott* burned hard, and that night she was supposed to be sunk by a destroyer, but four torpedoes did not put her down. She burned, a beacon for the enemy that night.

True to his promise, Admiral Fletcher moved out with his carriers at the end of the second day, despite the protests of Admiral Turner and General Vandegrift. Because the carriers were not there, and also because of the results of the naval battle of Savo Island a few hours later, the marines found themselves isolated on Guadalcanal, facing a superior naval force and the powerful Japanese naval air force. For a time the U.S. was very near to losing its slender grip on the island, largely because of Admiral Fletcher's intractability.

What followed is described in the next volume of this series, *South Pacific*.

NOTES

The material for the preamble comes from the records of CINCPAC in the Operational Archives of the Navy Historical Center in Washington, D.C. The success of Admiral Wilson Brown's raid on Japanese forces at Lae and Salamaua was not known to the Americans at the time, but it caused a change in Japanese strategy and much more care in the resupply of Japanese forces in New Guinea.

1 The "Victory Disease"

The material for this chapter comes from a series of interviews with Lieutenant General Jimmy Doolittle and from Commander Edwin T. Layton's book *And I Was There*. The material about the Japanese plans comes from the Japanese official war history. The material about Admiral Frank Jack Fletcher comes from his operational report on the Coral Sea battle.

2 Tulag: Landing

The poem "Remember December the Eighth" comes from the *Japan Times* of December 15, 1941. The material about Admiral Isoroku Yamamoto's antipathy for Admiral Chuichi Nagumo is from Eichi Sorimachi's biography of Admiral Yamamoto. The material about the movements of the *Lexington* is from the CINCPAC files and from a long interview with Admiral Aubrey W. Fitch. The story of the Battle of the Coral Sea comes from the CINCPAC files and various action reports of the carriers and their air squadrons. The note about Admiral Fletcher's dislike of radio intelligence is from Commander Layton's book, *And I Was There*.

3 Score: Japan 2—U.S. 1

The continuing story of the Battle of the Coral Sea is from the Japanese and American naval records and the interview with Admiral Fitch. The quotation from Admiral Fletcher is from Commander Layton's book. The story of Admiral Yamamoto and the reactions of the Japanese admirals is from materials gathered for my biography of Admiral Yamamoto, interviews, and the Japanese naval history files. The tale about Admiral Matome Ugaki is from his diary, published in Japan in Japanese after the war.

4 The Carriers Attack

The details of the battle of the Coral Sea are from the naval records and the Japanese records. The story of the struggle to save the *Lexington* comes from the action report of Admiral Fitch.

5 Nimitz Smells Something Fishy

The note about the attitude of the Japanese comes from my reading the Japanese newspapers of the period. The story of the discovery of the Japanese target of Midway is from W. J. Holmes' *Double Edged Secrets*. The material about Colonel Kiyonao Ichiki is from the Japanese army records and my study of Admiral Yamamoto's life. The story of the impending battle of Midway is from the American naval records and the Japanese official war history.

6 Nagumo Prepares

The material about Admiral Nagumo is from the official Japanese war history. Commander Layton's book was also useful.

7 Nagumo Attacks

Midway by Commanders Mitsuo Fuchida and Masatake Okumiya was valuable for this part of the book. So was Commander Layton's book, as well as the official Japanese war history volume on Midway. The records of CINCPAC were used for the American story.

8 Counterattack and Check

Samuel Eliot Morison's books on Midway and on the Aleutians were useful here, as was the Fuchida-Okumiya book.

9 The Americans Move

This chapter comes from Admiral Raymond Spruance's action report on the Battle of Midway and from the Japanese official war history. The material about Commander John C. Waldron is from Frederick Mears' *Carrier Combat*. The Kusaka story is from his interview with the U.S. Strategic Bombing Survey.

10 Getting Back

This chapter relied heavily on Admiral Spruance's action report of the Midway battle.

11 Nagumo Strikes Back

The story of the Japanese reaction is from the Fuchida-Okumiya book and from the Japanese official war history.

12 The Last Air Attack

Admiral Ugaki's diary was valuable for this story of what happened to the Japanese at Midway. The Fuchida-Okumiya book was important as well, and the CINCPAC records tell the American story.

13 The Sinking of the *Yorktown*

The story of the sinking of the *Yorktown* is from the CINCPAC records. The story of Admiral Spruance's operations is from his action report and from an interview with Rear Admiral Carl J. Moore, Spruance's long-time chief of staff.

14 The Meaning of Midway
The analysis of Midway comes from the Fuchida-Okumiya book and from my own observations.

15 The Aleutians
The story of the battle for the Aleutians is from the Japanese official war history and from Samuel Eliot Morison's Volume 7: *Aleutians, Gilberts and Marshalls*.

16 Troubles at Home
The material about life in Japan comes from several sources, most particularly the *Japan Times* of the period and *Asahi Shimbun*, which was then the biggest Japanese daily newspaper.

17 Remnants and Rovers
The story of the submarine *Trout* is from the records of the Pacific Fleet and materials in the Pacific Fleet Submarine Museum at Pearl Harbor. The material about the faulty American torpedo firing mechanism comes from an interview with Admiral Ralph Christie.

18 China, the Attrition War
The material for this chapter on the China war comes from my own experience as a correspondent in China during the war.

19 The Aleutian Seas
The story of the battle of the Aleutians is from Samuel Eliot Morison's Volume 7 and the CINCPAC records.

20 Planning the Offensive
This chapter relied heavily on the records of the King-Nimitz meetings, which occurred every few months, usually in San Francisco; the CINCPAC records; and the biographies of General Douglas MacArthur.

21 Operation Shoestring
This chapter depended on General Samuel B. Griffiths' book, *The Battle for Guadalcanal*, and Samuel Eliot Morison's Volume 5: *The Struggle for Guadalcanal*. *The Amphibians Came to Conquer*, Admiral George Dyer's book about Admiral Richmond Kelly Turner, was also valuable.

22 Guadalcanal Landing
The story of the Guadalcanal landings is from the action reports of the Pacific Fleet as well as from the books of Admiral Dyer, General Griffiths, and Samuel Eliot Morison.

BIBLIOGRAPHY

Agawa, Horyuki. *The Reluctant Admiral*. Tokyo: Kodansha, 1979.

Boei Senshi Shitsu, Senshi Shos. The official Japanese Defense Agency history of the Pacific War (100 vols.). Tokyo: undated.

Dyer, George. *The Amphibians Came to Conquer*. Washington, D.C.: U.S. Navy, undated.

Griffiths, Samuel B. *The Battle for Guadalcanal*. New York: Bantam Books, 1980.

Hoyt, Edwin P. *Blue Skies and Blood, the Battle of the Coral Sea*. New York: Paul S. Eriksson, Publisher, 1975.

Ienaga, Saburo. *The Pacific War, 1937–1945*. New York: Pantheon Books, 1978.

Ito, Masanori. *The End of the Imperial Japanese Navy*. New York: W.W. Norton & Co., 1956.

Johnston, Stanley. *Queen of the Flattops*. New York: E.P. Dutton, 1942.

Layton, Edwin T. *And I Was There*. New York: William Morrow and Company, 1985.

Li, Lincoln. *The Japanese Army in North China, 1937–1941*. Tokyo: Oxford University in Asia, 1975.

Mears, Frederick. *Carrier Combat*. New York: Doubleday, 1944.

Morison, Samuel Eliot. *History of United States Naval Operations in World War II*. Boston: Atlantic, Little Brown, 1947–1975.
> Vol. 1 *The Rising Sun in the Pacific*
> Vol. 4 *Coral Sea, Midway, and Submarine Actions*
> Vol. 5 *The Struggle for Guadalcanal*
> Vol. 7 *Aleutians, Gilberts and Marshalls*

Overy, R.J. *The Air War, 1939–1945*. New York: Stein and Day, 1981.

Prange, Gordon. *Miracle at Midway*. New York: McGraw Hill, 1982.

Wolfert, Ira. *The Battle of the Solomons*. Boston: Houghton Mifflin Company, 1943.

INDEX

Abe, Jiroaki, 91, 101
Abe, Koso, 29
Abele, T. C., 52
Adak, 124, 125
Adams, 174
Admiralties, 139
Agriculture production, Japanese, 129–130
Alchi 99 dive-bombers, 35
Aircraft production: Japanese, 129; U.S., 128
Akagi, 30, 52, 57, 60, 61, 62, 63, 64, 68, 71, 72, 75, 83, 84, 91, 92, 94, 99, 114; and attack on, 85—86; and damage to, 87–88
Akebono Maru, 78; and attack on, 54
Alaska Peninsula, 122
Alaskan Defense Command (U.S.), 122
Alaskan operation, 55–56
Alaskan Sector of the Thirteenth Naval District (U.S.), 122
Aleutian Islands, 121–126; operations, 42
Aleutian Seas, 149
Amagai, Commander, 92, 93
Amchitka Island, 150
American Division in New Caledonia, 156
Anderson, 37
Aoki, Captain, 57–58
Arare, 150
Arashiuo, 109
Astoria, 96, 110
Athenia, 134
Attack Method C, 103
Attu Island, 125, 150, 153; and battle of, 126
Ault, W. B., 5
Australia, 156
Azgattu Island, 151

B-16 aircraft, 66
B-17 aircraft, 19, 54, 66, 71, 78
B-26 aircraft, 67–68
Baldwin, Hanson, 39
Beach Blue, 171
Benham, 111
Bismarck Archipelago, 144
Bombing Five, 32
Bose, Subhas Chandra, 14
Brockman, W. H., Jr., 93
Brown, F. E., 145
Brown, Wilson, 2, 3, 4, 5
Browning, Miles W., 79–80, 81
Buchanan, 174
Buckmaster, Captain, 111
Buckner, Simon Bolivar, 122
Buka Island, 157
Burch, W. O., 16
Bureau of Ordnance, 142
Burma, 147

Calcutta Maru, 137
Callaghan, Admiral, 166
Cape Esperance, 167
Carpender, Arthur S., 159
Carrier Division Five (Japan), 10
Carrier Division Two: *See Hiryu*, *Soryu*
Carrier doctrine: Japanese, 81; U.S., 81
Cates, C. B., 169
Central Pacific submarines, 143
Charleston, 122
Chicago, 175
Chichagof, 125
Chikuma, 57, 61, 62, 104, 116
China, 147–148
Ching-wei, Wang, 147
Chitose, 48, 103
Chochalousek, W. G., 89
Christie, Ralph, 141, 142
Chungking, 147

181